SIX CHAPTERS OF
LIFE IN A CADRE SCHOOL

Also of Interest

† Available in hardcover and paperback.

About the Book and Author

Yang Chiang's *Six Chapters of Life in a Cadre School* is a memoir of her two years of "reeducation" in the countryside during China's Cultural Revolution. A research fellow with the Chinese Academy of Social Sciences, Yang Chiang studied Western literature at Oxford in the early 1930s and spent some time in Paris and Berlin. Before the Communist Revolution, she had been well known as a playwright and literary critic but afterward focused primarily on research work. In 1970, she was sent to a cadre school in Honan.

Bypassing discussion of sensitive topics, the author focuses on daily happenings. Through seemingly irrelevant and minute details—the process of digging a well, clandestine visits with her husband, getting treatment for minor ailments, the puppy that she adopts—the author allows the reader to figure out the hidden meaning that she is trying to convey. Her chronicle of these mundane activities contains no complaints or polemics but is rather a telling commentary on the governmental system and its bureaucrats. What is left unsaid speaks louder than what is said.

Six Chapters of Life in a Cadre School was written during a brief liberalization period in the late 1970s and was published in Hong Kong in 1981. Within a few months it was republished both in China and Taiwan, a rare phenomenon in these politically sensitive times. There have been several translations into English, French, and Japanese, attesting to its popularity among non-Chinese readers. For this edition, the translator has provided extensive notes to clarify passages that would be obscure for Western readers and to explain the implications of literary references made by the author.

The translator, Djang Chu, is associate director and coordinator of academic affairs at the Institute of Asian Studies, St. John's University.

SIX CHAPTERS OF LIFE IN A CADRE SCHOOL

Memoirs from China's Cultural Revolution

幹校六記

Yang Chiang,
Translated and Annotated by Djang Chu

楊　絳

章　楚

Westview Press / Boulder and London

Copyright © 1986 by Westview Press, Inc.

Published in 1986 in the United States of America by Westview Press, Inc.; Frederick A. Praeger, Publisher; 5500 Central Avenue, Boulder, Colorado 80301

Library of Congress Cataloging in Publication Data
Yang, Chiang.
    Six chapters of life in a cadre school.
    Translation of: Kan-hsiao liu-chi.
    1. Yang, Chiang—Biography. 2. China—History—
Cultural Revolution, 1966–1969. 3. Authors, Chinese—
20th century—Biography. I. Djang, Chu. II. Title.
PS2922.C49Z46813 1986   895.1'8509 [B]   85-13924
ISBN 0-8133-7099-X

This book has been produced without formal editing by the publisher
Composition for this book was provided by the translator
Printed and bound in the United States of America

10   9   8   7   6   5   4   3   2   1

Contents

Translator's Introduction

During the Cultural Revolution Chinese intellectuals on the mainland were effectively silenced by endless cycles of political movements launched by the Communist authorities. When the "emancipation of the mind" movement was inaugurated by political moderates in the late seventies immediately after the death of Mao, artists and writers jumped at the opportunity to vent their long-suppressed sentiments. Beethoven was played by the Peking symphony orchestra; impressionist artists were allowed to display their works in public; and in literature, a new realism that dared to speak against the injustices of China's socialist society became a popular trend. This so-called "exposé literature" was tolerated because the leadership was anxious to enlist the support of intellectuals in discrediting and weeding out the remaining leftist deviationists of the Cultural Revolution—a practical and ingenious application of the maxim of "literature serving politics." The new realism in literature, however, went beyond the recalling of past bitterness; it also revealed the weaknesses of China's social system.

Six Chapters of Life in a Cadre School by Yang Chiang is an outstanding piece of literature published during the second blooming of the "hundred flowers." It will be recalled that in 1957 Mao raised the campaign slogan: "Let a hundred flowers bloom and a hundred schools of thought contend," an invitation to non-Communist intellectuals to express whatever was on their minds. But soon the criticisms became far more sharp and biting than Mao had expected. He felt it necessary to silence the critics and publicly denounce them as "rightists." Thus ended the first blooming of the hundred flowers. This, of course, was an outrageous violation of the pledge of immunity that had been given the intellectuals. China's intelligentsia was thus taught a lesson—that "blooming and contending" was dangerous and should be avoided. By the time the Party and Government began to re-evaluate what had happened during the so-called "lost decade," a few people found the courage to completely expose past deceit and atrocity, since Teng Hsiao-p'ing had repeatedly assured that the hundred flowers atmosphere would continue, albeit with provisos requiring support of socialism and promotion of the four modernizations.

Six Chapters is a personal account of what happened in a cadre school, an institution established during the Cultural Revolution for the purpose of re-educating intellectuals. It is a story simply stated, without toting up dead bodies and horror stories or launching into emotional outbursts. But between the lines the reader can sense that the author has been emotionally lacerated by her savage indignation.

Yang Chiang is a research fellow of the Foreign Language Section of the Philosophy and Social Sciences Research Department of the Chinese Academy of Sciences. Also a noted playwright and storyteller, she managed to publish, during this relaxed period, a Chinese translation of *Don Quixote* in 1978 which is now in its third or fourth printing. Given the restrictions imposed on writers on the mainland, the tone of the *Six Chapters* is delightfully fresh and blatantly outspoken. Yang Chiang is the wife of Ch'ien Chung-shu, an outstanding scholar and novelist, whose satirical fiction *Wei-ch'eng* or *Fortress Besieged* had made international literary history overnight, and has been translated into English, French, Czech, and Russian. One can easily detect in Yang's book that touch of comic exuberance and bitter irony which so resembles the hallmark of Ch'ien Chung-shu's writing.

In November 1969 Ch'ien Chung-shu was "sent down" to a cadre school in Honan to remold his mental outlook through physical labor. Several months later, Yang Chiang was "sent down" to the same school, but they could not stay together as they belonged to different units. The term *hsia-fang*, or the "send down" movement has been variously translated as the "to the village," "back to the grass-roots," or "down to the countryside" movement. However, the phrase also embodies a broader meaning implying decentralization of power or degradation of social status. It was first used as early as 1942 in connection with the rectification movement during which intellectuals in Yenan were ordered to the countryside to engage in agricultural production and to immerse themselves in village life in order to avoid alienation from the peasant masses. Allegedly the movement was designed to overcome the traditional psychological barriers separating mental and manual labor, but it turned out to be a convenient way to punish ideological dissidents and to curb the burgeoning bureaucracy as well. *Hsia-fang* did not always involve physical labor; sometimes cadres were sent to rural areas to teach in village schools or to help in organizing party and government structures.

Toward the end of the Cultural Revolution when the usefulness of the Red Guards as street fighters was over, Mao decreed that these revolutionary youths should be "sent up to the mountains and down to the villages" to help agricultural production and to learn from the peasant masses. No less than seventeen million urban youths were thus rusticated. No matter how high-sounding and attractive the movement appeared in its slogans, the youths sent down realized that it was in reality a form of camouflaged labor reform and perpetual banishment, similar to the traditional form of punishment meted out by the imperial court to criminals deserving something short of capital punishment. Mao had ingeniously borrowed the trappings of the old empire and paraded them as a socialist innovation.

Earlier, on May 7, 1966, Mao wrote a letter to Lin Piao, then his "closest comrade-in-arms," outlining his policy on "grasping revolution and promoting production." He declared that a political aim of the proletarian revolution was to make education serve socialist policies and be combined with labor. Thousands of May Seventh cadre schools sprang up overnight in rural areas to accommodate cadres from government offices, artists' and writers' associations, universities, and research organizations who were to be tempered and remolded to rid themselves of their prejudices against manual labor. Starting from the fall of 1969, huge numbers of government employees were dispatched in groups to cadre schools in rural areas with the hope that the supernumerary officials of the bloated bureaucracy in Peking would sweat out their bourgeois beliefs by an extended period of manual labor. Chou En-lai stated in 1970 that the number of cadres in the central administration had been cut from 60,000 to 10,000 during the Cultural Revolution's drive to remold intellectuals and streamline the administration. For instead of withering away as predicted by Marx, the state bureaucracy by then had reached unmanageable proportions. The *hsia-fang* movement, therefore, constituted an effective way to curb the effect of Parkinson's Law to which even a Communist regime was not automatically immune.

The style of the book is modelled after that of *Fu-sheng liu-chi* or *Six Chapters of a Floating Life*, a charming eighteenth century book by Shen Fu. As a genre of literature, *Six Chapters of a Floating Life* is unique in that it is a mixture of autobiographical accounts and observations on life, as well as criticisms on art and literature. The author's description of minor events in minute detail makes the book revealing and interesting. So far as social outlook is concerned, the author is a rebel who challenges the validity of tradition and openly defies it. Since Lin Yutang translated *Floating Life* into English and published it in *Tien-hsia* magazine in 1935, the book has received a good reception among intellectuals throughout the English-speaking world.

Six Chapters of Life in a Cadre School follows the technique used in *Floating Life* in that it makes no flat statements, but describes seemingly irrelevant and minute events, thus allowing the reader to figure out the hidden meaning the author has tried to convey. There is no criticism of the social system per se; occasionally there are romantic and positive clichés about the monolithic Communist regime. The author does not challenge Mao's verdict concerning the intellectuals who were indeed alienated from the masses, but she doubts whether the peasant masses could teach them anything at all. One wonders if the original Maoist vision was really an unmitigated disaster. The cadre school, after all, was not unlike a summer camp for adults, and served to keep intellectuals physically fit and mentally alert. It was only the compulsory element and bureaucratic bungling that made it repulsive. In the final analysis, it is the gap separating the officially proclaimed morality and the venal reality of the situation that creates the subdued cynicism. In her descriptions of the cadre school, there is nothing even remotely resembling that of the Gulag Archipelago; it is a battered ideology and social structure that submerges the individual in the group, and the central question focuses on the relationship of the individual versus the all-powerful state. The book, in the main, could be read as a footnote to the sorry history of the now thoroughly discredited Cultural Revolution.

There is one aspect of the book which, however, has been ignored by most readers. Its quality as a tale of love is overshadowed by its social and political implications. Like its predecessor, *Floating Life,* a story of married love and of tribulations sustained in real life, *Six Chapters* shows great tenderness and devotion between an elderly husband and wife throughout numerous difficulties—in the agony of separation, in the attempt to keep tragic news from each other, in the joy of stealing a few moments together during working hours and in the clandestine visits made in dark snowy nights. Perhaps the author had intended her book to be a testimony of their enduring love as well as an indictment of the irrational social system of the time.

In order for the reader to obtain a fair picture of this period, he is advised to read this book together with Jack Chen's *A Year in Upper Felicity* (Macmillan Publishing Co., 1973) which describes life in a cadre school in Honan at approximately the same time. The latter contains nothing but positive stories, praising the virtues of socialist society. Most of it is written in stilted Marxist rhetoric similar to that of the *Peoples' Daily.* The author was an information officer of the Peking Publishing Bureau and wrote the book before the fall of the Gang of Four. Perhaps his motivation was simply one of political self-preservation. Chen's book presents a contrasting picture with the implied content of the *Six Chapters of Life in a Cadre School.*

Since its publication, *Six Chapters* has received acclamation from China experts throughout the world. "It shows a wound, yet utters no complaint," writes Simon Leys. Its underlying value as well as literary excellence, I think, lies in the fact that what is left unsaid speaks louder than what is said.

Admittedly, there are always two sides to a coin. The more pertinent question is what will be the image of Mao under the scrutiny of future historians? There is no question that Mao has carved a niche for himself in the annals of Chinese history. So far as the episode of the cadre schools is concerned, will Mao be remembered as a second Ch'in Shih-huang who buried hundreds of scholars alive, or as another Wang An-shih whose "socialist" policies were derailed by ignorant and incompetent subordinates?

My thanks are due to Ellen Klempner who did the editing, Sandra Esposito who typed the manuscript, Nora Shen who drew the illustrations, and my wife, Jane, who, as usual, offered criticisms, both relevant and irrelevant.

D. C.

ILLUSTRATIONS

下放幸引 Under a waving red flag, the veteran scholar Yü P'ing-po and his wife marched at the head of the column (p. 6).

鑿井記第

Ah-hsiang and I would go back to the kitchen and bring steamed bread, rice porridge, salted vegetables, and boiled water in a pushcart to the field to serve breakfast (p. 17).

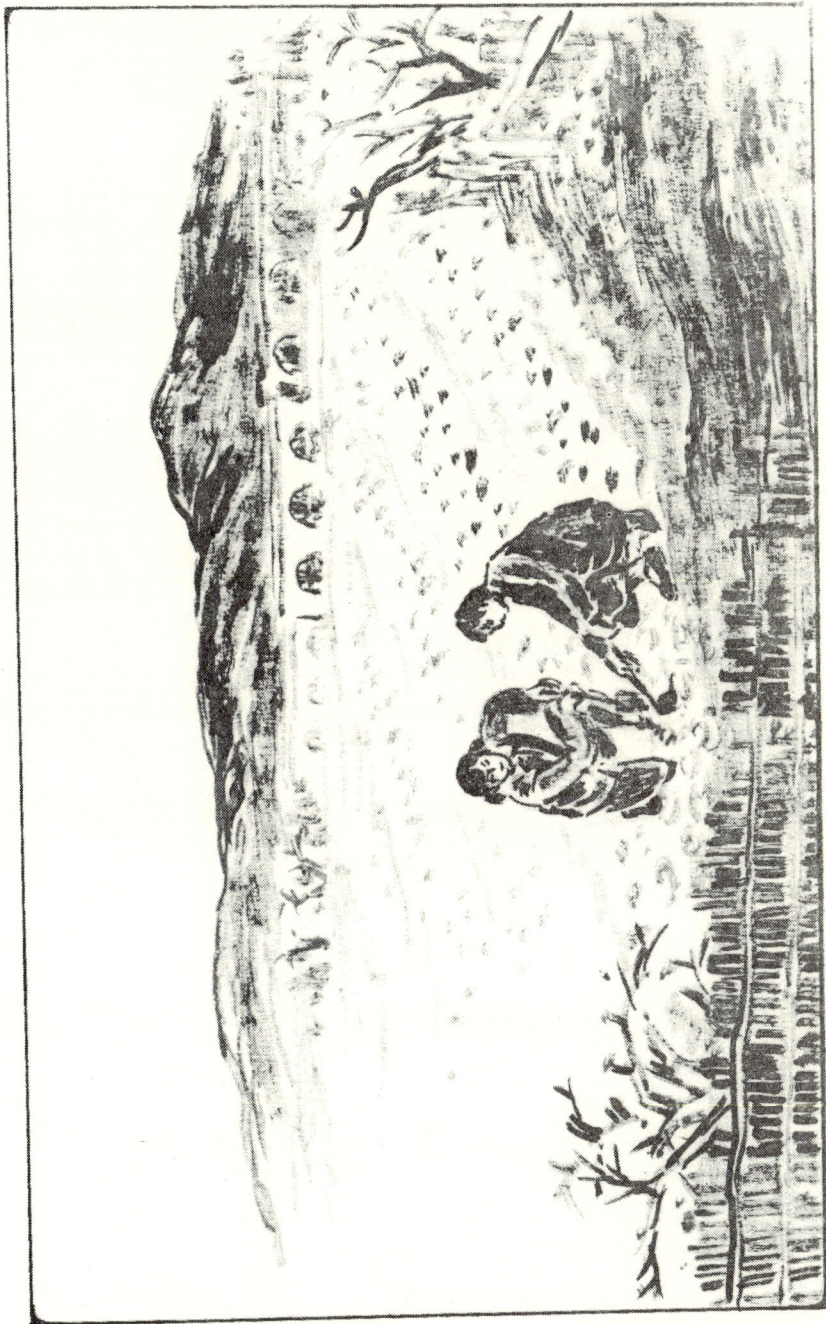

閑園記閑 When the weather turned cold, crouching in the field to weed and to loosen the soil was a tedious job. (p. 24)

小慧記情 Little Runner could not give me protection. Instead, I had to protect her, because in the short span of three months she had grown from a puppy to a "junior miss" dog (p. 40).

冒險記事本　I veered toward the west and after a while found the bridge (p. 57).

When we arrived at Ming-kang, fully expecting Meh-ts'un to be at the railway station waiting for us, we couldn't find him, either on the platform or on the road to the cadre school (p. 67).

Chapter 1

Departure at "Send Down" Time

The Academy of Social Sciences of which my husband Meh-ts'un[1] and I are members, was formerly called the Philosophy and Social Sciences Research Department of the Chinese Academy of Sciences, or just "Research Department" for short. My husband works in the literature section while I belong to the foreign language section. In 1969 when all intellectual workers were ordered by the authorities to undergo "re-education" by the Worker and Liberation Army Propaganda units,[2] we were organized into groups of various sizes, from six to ten fellow workers, each group occupying one room of the office as our living quarters. We performed physical exercise every morning. A day's work was divided into three study periods—morning, afternoon and evening sessions. After a little while, those who were deemed old or infirm were permitted to spend their nights at home. Later on, the study sessions were reduced to two, one in the morning and one in the afternoon. Meh-ts'un and I moved back to our home to spend the nights, but in the back of our minds, we knew that we wouldn't be able to stay together for long, for soon we would be "sent down" to the cadre schools. Although through a host of rumors, we had a vague idea about where the cadre schools would be, the date of departure, however, was not revealed. We could only speculate and wait.

Every day we had to line up to buy meals at the cafeterias of our respective units. The time we spent on these lines was tremendous, at least half an hour each time, but having meals at home was too troublesome and time-consuming, so when supervision of the propaganda units became less stringent, we often made arrangements to have our noon meals at a small restaurant. Although the food at the restaurant was no better than that of the cafeterias and the waiting time was not any shorter, by waiting together the chore seemed less tedious and it afforded us a chance to talk to each other.

On November 3, 1969, while waiting at a bus stop in front of the Research Department, I caught a glimpse of Meh-ts'un emerging from a crowd of passengers. He came over to me and whispered in my ear, "I have important news to tell you later." I couldn't make out what it was all about by the expression on his face.

After we squeezed aboard the bus, Meh-ts'un told me, "I'm going on the eleventh of this month. I belong to the vanguard group."

Although we had been waiting for this for some time, the news struck me like a bolt of lightning. Meh-ts'un's sixtieth birthday by Chinese reckoning was not far away and we had planned to celebrate by eating "long-life noodles." We figured that we could not possibly have the good fortune of celebrating his seventieth birthday. Now he was destined to be "sent down" just a few days before his sixtieth!

"But why are you assigned to the vanguard group?" I asked in desperation.

"Because of you," he answered in a matter-of-fact way. "Other people have to bring their families or make arrangements for them before they leave. You are supposedly capable of taking care of the family by yourself." It turned out that the cadre school to which Meh-ts'un had been assigned was located in Lo-shan, Honan province. All members of his section, except those in the vanguard group, were destined to depart on the seventeenth of November.

When we arrived at the restaurant that day, we ordered a ready-cooked dish of cut-up chicken in a crockery pot.

The dish was a disappointment, consisting of a few pieces of chicken bones and burned skin. I managed to mix some soup in a half bowl of rice, but I couldn't swallow anything.

We had only one week to prepare for Meh-ts'un's departure. He could not take leave until the last couple of days before then. On the pretext of having to make preparations I played truant from the office for a few days. This time the "send down" process was euphemistically called "moving with pots and pans"—this meant that people had to bring along all their earthly possessions, as if there would be no chance for them to come back again. Everyone carried a mountain of baggage—useless things and outworn clothing as well as treasured books and notes, etc. Our daughter, Ah-yüan, and her husband, Teh-i, were busy at work in their respective factories and could not spare much time. They finally came over on their day off to help us pack. Imitating what other people had done, we bound trunks and suitcases with heavy twine several times over for fear they might be crushed and broken on the journey. Alas, only wooden or sheet-metal containers could be protected this way. The human body seems to be capable of enduring more rough handling and harsh treatment than these containers.

Readiness to accept punishment was the essence of physical training and character forging. At the moment there was nothing else to prepare for other than this understanding. Selecting clothes to bring, however, presented a problem. If one's clothes were too old, they would not last. If they were brand new, they would be difficult to wash. I had long forsaken the use of the sewing machine, but now I found myself making a cover for Meh-ts'un's blanket with a piece of soil-resistant material, so that frequent washing could be avoided. I also darned a pair of his trousers with crisscross stitches on the seat so that it looked like a globe model with vertical and horizontal lines. Meh-ts'un said jokingly that the pants were equipped with a portable cushion, like the shell of a tortoise, and that it would be convenient for the wearer to sit down anywhere he chose. He said optimistically, "Don't spend too much energy on making preparations. When you are 'sent down,' we'll be able to take care of one another. As to the prospect of family reunion, we'll wait until Ah-yüan and her husband settle down in a rural area and send for us."

Soon the date of departure of the vanguard group, November 11, arrived. Ah-yüan, her husband and I were the only ones there to bid him farewell. As Meh-ts'un did not carry too much baggage, we found a place to rest for a while before he boarded the train. The waiting room was packed with people, talking, yelling and running every which way. The leader of the vanguard group dashed around like a chicken with its head cut off, and seemed to wish he could be in several places at once. Those who were over-burdened with baggage regretted that they did not have more hands to handle the parcels. Out of generosity, Teh-i put down what he was carrying and offered to help others. Meh-ts'un and I felt gratified, deeming it an encouraging sign of the new society. At the same time, we comforted each other with the knowledge that Ah-yüan was fortunate to have such a kind-hearted life companion—we could feel at ease about her future.

While Teh-i grasped other people's luggage, we carried our own small parcels and bags. Following the line, we pushed ourselves onto the platform and then onto the train. As soon as Meh-ts'un found a seat, we retreated from the train and waited patiently for it to start.

In my mind I recalled how people in days gone by would go abroad on huge oceanliners. First, as they boarded a launch which took them to the liner, their friends and relatives threw coils of colored paper streamers at them to hold. As the launch chugged away slowly from the shore, the multi-colored paper streamers broke one by one amidst the shouts and applause of those who stood on the shore. Among the merrymakers there were people who wept furtively as if their hearts had broken along with the severing of the colored streamers. If the feelings of parting and separation of those who were going to the cadre schools on the train and their relatives and friends on the platform were visible that day, they were certainly not multi-colored, nor could they be broken as easily as paper streamers.

Meh-ts'un came to the door of the train and told us to go home. "Don't wait for the train to start," he said. We looked at each other from a distance, speechless and depressed. "Let him see the three of us going back together," I said to myself, "to spare him the unnecessary worry of seeing the sad expressions on our faces as the train pulls out." So we left without waiting for the train to start, looking back several times as we walked. The platform was still crowded with humanity and the train remained immobile. We arrived home in low spirits. Ah-yüan and Teh-i had to go back to their factories. They were schoolmates, but had not studied in the same department and worked in different factories.

Two days later, the office of the literature section sent word that those who had gone to cadre schools could bring their own beds and that they should be dismantled and tied up properly with twine and delivered to the Research Department immediately. To dismantle a bed and tie the pieces up with heavy twine was a job which could not be accomplished singlehandedly. The difficulty was that heavy twine is not amenable to making knots, and that the ends of the twine must be tucked away securely underneath the loops. I had only one more day of leave and was alone at home. I tackled the job by first dismantling a small bed and dividing it up into several sections. Trying to tie up the sections together, I found that it was impossible without the help of a third hand. I had to enlist the service of my teeth and bit hard into a piece of string which was attached to the twine. Thus, the bed sections were tied up in three separate bundles; to each was attached a label with Meh-ts'un's name written on it. I was afraid that the sections of the bed would get lost, like members of a refugee family during a military upheaval. Luckily, Meh-ts'un reported later in a letter that the bed had arrived safely and that none of the sections had gone astray, although considerable time had been spent in locating them.

The members of the literature section and those of another section were the first to be "sent down." Each section was now called a "company," borrowing the appellations of the

military. On the day of departure of these two companies,
workers of the Research Department staged an elaborate
send-off ceremony with drums beating and gongs sounding.
The office declared it a holiday and all of us were required
to participate. The people being "sent down" marched out
in a neat column. Under a billowing red flag, the veteran
scholar Master Yü P'ing-po[3] and his wife marched at the
head of the column. Both were well over seventy years old,
yet like small school children they were being "sent down"
to the cadre schools to undergo re-education. I could not
stand the sight of it and left early. On the way back I met
several colleagues who displayed little enthusiasm for the
send-off affair. They preferred to go back to the office to
work rather than attend the tragi-comical spectacle. Their
faces were devoid of any expression.

While we were waiting to be "sent down" to the cadre
schools to remold ourselves, we did not have the inclination
to savor that "peculiar, melancholy sentiment of departure"
celebrated in a poem by the Emperor of the Southern T'ang
dynasty.[4] Ever since a portion of the colleagues of the Research
Department had gone to the cadre schools, we who remained
had to redouble our efforts at remolding, so we studied hard
day and night. Even our worker-teacher who was responsible
for our re-education became tired of it. Our youthful instructor, no more than twenty-three years of age, said indignantly, "I've wrought iron in front of the furnace everyday
and never felt tired. Now, I sit here from morning to night—
my buttocks ache, my head throbs, and my whole body is
drained of energy." Evidently forging human beings is more
difficult than tempering steel. "Sitting on a cold bench" to
teach others is a demanding job.

Forging human beings demanded the imposition of cease-
less physical exercise. After we finished digging the air raid
shelter—a labyrinthian underground structure—we worked
on a project which consisted of moving library books from
one building to another and from upstairs to downstairs.
The job demanded sorting out, bundling up, transporting
and arranging books on the shelves. After we finished moving
the books of our unit, we moved books of other units. One

day we carried books, cabinets and bookshelves out of a room which was needed for immediate occupancy. The books had been untouched for three years and the shelves were covered with a thick layer of dust. One colleague sneezed more than twenty times as soon as he stepped into that room. Even with the use of filter masks, our faces were powdered with dust. We coughed up greyish phlegm when we completed our assignment. I remembered that it was the time of the year when cold morning weather would suddenly turn warm and then hot at noon. The work of moving metal shelves, bookcases and filing cabinets—with drawers full of catalogue cards—was done by younger colleagues who carried these objects on their shoulders. The rough surfaces of their burdens tore their shirts, exposing their bare flesh. It dawned on me that the human body could withstand the toughest punishment in the world.

As the saying goes, the meek are the blessed of the earth. I did only minor and insignificant chores. Whenever I had spare time, I managed to get parcels ready to be sent to Meh-ts'un. Meh-ts'un, on the other hand, used whatever leisure he had to write letters to me. The letters were short and haphazardly written, usually composed of only a few sentences. Some were written during the day and others at night. If only we had kept these letters, it would be fun to read them again today. But more valuable and important correspondence had also been lost; the loss of these letters is not worth mentioning.

I learned that when the vanguard unit went to the cadre school, the first thing they did was to clean up an unoccupied and dusty "reform-by-labor camp." The first night they slept on straw mats and felt warm and comfortable, but it snowed heavily soon afterwards. The ground became muddy and the weather turned bitter cold. The main force of the literature section arrived on the seventeenth. No less than eighty male workers were confined in one big room where everyone slept on a communal brick-bed. One unruly brat who had been sent down with his father had the bad habit of bed-wetting, and often gave his bedfellows in the vicinity a thorough "fertilization." On their day off they went to the town to buy delicacies—roast chicken and cooked tortoises. I asked Meh-ts'un how the tortoise tasted. He replied that he hadn't had the courage to try it, but he surreptitiously composed a few humorous ditties and had them mailed to me.

There was no arable land to be found in Lo-shan. Thus the students of the cadre school had nothing to do. After one month, the whole school and its dependants together with their baggage, which was considerable, moved to Tung-yo Village of Hsi-hsien. Hsi-hsien could be found on the map, however Tung-yo could not. It was a miserable and sparsely populated place, where lack of fuel made life unbearable in the winter. Many female colleagues acquired chilblains on their faces. Washing clothes by pounding them was performed at the edge of a pond. Meh-ts'un had to beg a village woman to wash his new shirts for him, but some of them mysteriously disappeared in the process. I was afraid that he might fall into the pond if he tried to do it himself. So long as he had someone to do it for him, the loss of a few shirts was immaterial.

Those who were waiting to be "sent down" were naturally anxious to know about the daily life in the cadre school. I was often asked to reveal what little information I had gathered. One of the stories I told proved to be most popular—that was the fish story of Ho Ch'i-fang.[5] One day the local people had drained a pond and caught some fish, so the cadre school canteen menu now offered red-cooked fish. This was commendable because it proved that the authorities were determined to improve the diet of its charges. Ho Ch'i-fang hurriedly took his enamel toilet mug to the canteen and bought a portion of fish, but was puzzled by the strange taste of this delicacy. Upon investigation, he found a piece of half dissolved medicated soap at the bottom of the mug. Apparently, he had been in such a haste to eat fish that he had forgotten to look into the mug. Everyone enjoyed the story which evoked a great deal of laughter each time it was told. In return, they told a story about my husband. The story was that Ch'ien Chung-shu and a certain comrade Ting, both senior research fellows, had been instructed to boil water on an open hearth. However, even after working at it conscientiously for half a day, they could not bring the water to a boil. I was not amused. "The hearth is in open air," I said in their defense. "It's not easy to bring water to a boil against strong wind and heavy snow." But the story of my husband boiling water stuck.

The members of the literature section started to build their own living quarters at the beginning of the year. Even female comrades participated as able-bodied laborers in the work of pulling carts, making moulds, firing bricks and building houses. Only Meh-ts'un and others like Mr. Yü P'ing-po who had been categorized as old, infirm or disabled were spared of hard work. Instead they did miscellaneous jobs which required no physical strength. Eight months after they were "sent down," the company to which I belonged was dispatched to the cadre school. By that time they had already moved to the new living quarters they had built with their own hands.

Our company departed from Peking on July 12, 1970. When Meh-ts'un left eight months ago, the three of us— Teh-i, Ah-yüan and I had seen him off. This time when I departed only Ah-yüan came to the station. Her husband, Teh-i, had committed suicide a month earlier.

Teh-i had admitted to me that his ideology was a little inclined to the right, and that he could not stand the hypocrisy of the radical leftists. When the university he attended started a campaign for the extermination of the 516 group,[6] a few leftists who were under suspicion of being members confessed falsely that Teh-i was their organizer and that he had a name-list of the group. At that time, Teh-i had returned to the university, while Ah-yüan still remained in the factory. They could not come home on the same day of the week. When Teh-i left home for the last time, he said "Mom, I cannot offend the masses and I cannot take a belligerent attitude toward the Workers' Propaganda Unit. But I certainly will not draw up a fictitious list of names to destroy others. I have never lied before." When he returned to the university, he lost his freedom. Class struggle sessions were carried to a frenzied crescendo with threats of hell-fire and brimstone exploding all over the campus. Under the leadership of the Workers' Propaganda Unit, the activists of his department divided themselves into three groups to struggle against Teh-i by turn everyday with the goal of obtaining the nonexistent name-list. Seeking an easy way out, Teh-i committed suicide.

After I boarded the train that day, I told Ah-yüan not to wait for the train to start. She was by nature not sentimental and was endowed with a strong character. I could leave her without undue concern. But when I caught a glimpse of her back as she walked hesitantly toward the gate alone, I felt as if my heart had been stabbed with a dagger. I closed my eyes quickly. But behind closed eyes I visualized her rearranging the broken, disordered home of ours without Teh-i. Quickly I reopened my eyes; she had already gone and I could not see her through the train window. I had to keep my eyes closed to swallow my tears as the train slowly started to move. And that's how I left Peking.

I met Meh-ts'un at the cadre school. He was darker and thinner than before, and looked almost like a total stranger. But surprisingly I could still recognize him.

There was a Doctor Huang in the cadre school who was a person warm at heart and rather uninhibited with her words. Once Meh-ts'un visited her clinic for treatment of a minor ailment and registered under his real name, Ch'ien Chung-shu. Dr. Huang became angry, saying, "You're an imposter. I know Ch'ien Chung-shu and you are certainly not him." Meh-ts'un assured her that he was the genuine Ch'ien Chung-shu. "I know Ch'ien Chung-shu's lover too,"[7] Dr. Huang said. Meh-ts'un was not intimidated and had the guts to stand this test. He told her my name. Dr. Huang was still unconvinced and expressed her doubts. Meh-ts'un rationalized to himself that as a patient even an imposter would receive the same treatment, so he stopped arguing with her. Later I met Dr. Huang and reminded her of the story. Bursting into laughter, she said, "How come he had changed so completely?"

I can't remember exactly how Meh-ts'un looked and what clothes he had on when we met at the cadre school. I only remember that he had a red boil on his right cheek. The size of the boil was no bigger than a hazelnut, but it had a menacing look. A bright red color crowned the top and a dull yellow circled the surrounding area. Evidently there was pus inside. I exclaimed, "That's a carbuncle! What you need is a hot compress." But who was there to administer that to him? I saw soiled fingerprints all over the clinic's emergency kits, gauze rolls and cotton balls. Meh-ts'un said that he had had a similar boil some time ago. The authorities had permitted him to rest for a few days and spared him from the job of looking after the stove. His current assignment was looking after tools and performing nightwatchman's duty at night. His immediate supervisor had granted him a leave of half a day to accommodate my visit. But the leader of my company, being very strict, allowed me time only for a brief meeting and told me to return to the company immediately. Meh-ts'un accompanied me on my return journey and we parted without much being said. Ah-yüan and I had agreed to hide the news of Teh-i's suicide from him for the time being. After a few days, he wrote me to say that the boil turned out to be a carbuncle and that there were five pussy lesions. But after a few injections, the infection had subsided.

Although we were separated by a distance which could be covered by an hour's walk, we belonged to different companies and could not meet often. We both had to obey orders and observe strict discipline. Although we could not visit each other, we kept up a regular correspondence. Only on our day off could we meet openly. However, our day off did not fall on Sunday. Every ten days we had one day off which was called "Big Sunday." But when there was important business, "Big Sunday" could be cancelled. Still, compared with Ah-yüan who lived in Peking alone, we were fortunate to be living so close to each other.

Chapter 2

Hard Work Digging a Well

Work at the cadre school involved several different kinds of physical labor. Wheat and legume raising was the major form of field work. During summer days, members got up at three o'clock in the morning and went to the fields on empty stomachs, as breakfast was not brought to them till six o'clock. After breakfast, they worked until the rest period at noon. Work started again in the late afternoon and lasted until dark.

When the members of the various companies first arrived, they stayed in local villagers' homes. But such arrangements could not last long, so we had to build our own houses. To build a house requires an abundance of bricks. But regular bricks were difficult to make, so we used mud bricks instead. Making mud bricks was a strenuous job. Hog raising, though not as strenuous, was dirty and tedious work. The old and the weak were assigned to kitchens or vegetable gardens, leaving the heavy work to the young and able-bodied colleagues.

One day the cadre school conducted a celebration meeting of some sort. All the items on the program were centered on the theme of the dignity and joy of labor. There was one skit depicting the bravery of a member of a company who redoubled his efforts to produce bricks despite the danger of working at an old, tottering kiln. It was said that the skit had been based on a true story. The members of a certain company presented an item on well drilling. The actors didn't say a single word throughout the performance. The only action involved performers pushing the handles of a drilling machine, while walking in endless circles to the rhythmic beat of "En yo . . . En yo . . . En yo . . ." Well drilling, in reality, was a job that got to be continuous, day and night, until the well was dug. In the skit, everyone pushed and walked in silence except for the sound of "En yo . . . En yo . . . En yo . . ." The low, deep penetrating sound was kept at a constant level, with no variation from beginning to end. It reminded me of the movie, "Volga Boatmen," which I had seen years before. In my mind, I visualized the heavy boots of the pulling gang dragging a heavily-laden boat step-by-step along the muddy bank of a river—only the feet, no faces.

In spite of its monotonous simplicity, the performance was more realistic and impressive than the kiln skit which publicized the virtues of labor with the message, "Don't be afraid of hardship and death." When the meeting was over, everyone said that the well drilling bit had been the best. It had required no rehearsal and was a simple daily routine put on the stage and transformed into a moving drama.

"Ah ya! . . . about this presentation . . .," someone exclaimed unthinkingly. "Is the ideology correct? There is a resemblance to . . . There is a resemblance to . . . We should . . . We should . . ."

Subtle smiles appeared on many faces. But suddenly, as if on cue, all the smiles were replaced by a stony silence. Everyone started to talk about other subjects.[8]

I was assigned to the vegetable garden team. We dug a well with bare hands without the benefit of a drilling machine.

The cadre school to which I belonged was on the bank of the Huai River, but as a matter of good fortune, the area had not suffered from flooding for two consecutive years. However, planting vegetables in dry and compact earth was something next to impossible. People say that the earth of Hsi-hsien is "a dish of paste when it rains and a sheet of copper when the sun shines." Our garden had been tilled by a tractor, but the machine had only dug up huge lumps of solidified mud, bigger than human heads and harder than bone. It was necessary to treat the mud lumps with infinite patience before vegetables could be planted. We had to break them and pulverize them which was a time-consuming job. After we have prepared the ground, we then dug an irrigation ditch, only to discover that there wasn't any water at all.

In a neighboring vegetable garden that also belonged to the cadre school, there was a machine-dug well, said to be ten meters deep. We often begged water from them for drinking purposes. Manually-dug wells could attain a depth of no more than three meters and the water was always turbid, so when we had to drink that water, we would pour in a bottle of anti-cholera lotion as a preventive measure. But it still tasted terrible. The water of the machine-dug well, however, was sweet and cool. Drinking a cup after heavy work quenched thirst like some kind of heavenly nectar. Whenever we could get hold of some of that water, we not only drank it, but washed our hands and feet with it as well. But if we wanted to use that water to irrigate our vegetable garden, it was almost impossible, as without the use of a pump, the well water could not reach our vegetable garden. Once after going through a great deal of red tape, we borrowed a pump. However, the water was largely absorbed or evaporated in our irrigation ditch before it reached a few patches of vegetables in the garden. Soon it became dark and we had to return the pump. Once we sowed some spinach seeds, but after one month there was still no sign of life. Only after a heavy downpour did there appear some greenish new growth. So we decided to dig a well no matter how much work it would entail. We selected a site and started to dig.

The ground was truly as hard as a polished copper plate. Wielding a heavy shovel, I dug with all my strength, but all I accomplished was to create a whitish mark on the ground. This evoked a ring of laughter among the younger members of the team. However, when it was their turn to dig, they found it just as difficult. Someone suggested that we use crane-bill–shaped shovels. Since I was famous for fast walking and my hands weren't of much help, I could put my feet to use. So I went back to the school at full speed to get

two crane-bill–shaped shovels. Putting them on my shoulders
I returned as fast as I could. The younger members dug the
ground by turn and the rest of us assisted in every way we
could. After a full day of hard work, we had dug a hole,
but there was no sign of water.

There was a young colleague nicknamed "Little Bull" who
was a male chauvinist. He whispered to someone standing
nearby, "You won't get water if you dig a well in the presence
of women." There were only two women on the vegetable
garden team. I was the oldest in the whole company. Ah-
hsiang, an overseas Chinese, was the youngest—she was
only half my age. Hearing this absurd statement, she was
incensed and told me so with indignation, and then lodged
a protest against "Little Bull." But neither of us was free
from worry. If there were no water, the blame would be put
squarely on us. Fortunately, before the hole we dug reached
the two-meter mark, the soil became wet and water did
emerge.

Digging dry ground was difficult, but handling wet soil
was even more arduous. The deeper we dug, the greater
amount of mire we encountered. Two or three barefoot young
men had to jump into the hole where they began to pass
up bucket after bucket of mud. Those standing above dumped
the contents onto the ground. Soon the hole was surrounded
by several inches of sticky loess. Everyone took off his or
her shoes and socks. Ah-hsiang, barefooted, handled the
buckets joyfully. I couldn't carry the buckets which were
too heavy for me, but to keep them company and in the
spirit of camaraderie, I also took off my shoes and socks.
Wielding a shovel, I tried to prevent the mud from spreading
all over the place.

I had always considered that mud was unclean and un-
healthy to touch, because it might contain human or animal
waste. But when I stuck my feet into it I felt a delectable
and comforting sensation—my "dirt phobia" was gone. It
was not unlike the way some people are able to overcome
their dread of a contagious disease by love for a relative
who has contracted it. Laughing to myself, I wondered

whether it could be that I had shifted my class stand, my philosophy of life.

We were afraid that if the hole was too full of water, it would be difficult to dig. Although manual digging was different from machine drilling which must be continuous to the end, we could not slacken our efforts at this critical moment. Emulating those who were doing the major field work, we would arrive at the digging site early in the morning every day on empty stomachs and start digging. Ah-hsiang and I would go back to the kitchen and bring steamed bread, rice porridge, salted vegetables and boiled water in a pushcart to the field to serve breakfast. I would push the cart on level ground and downhill slopes, while Ah-hsiang would push it on winding roads and uphill slopes. Her job was irksome as well as exhausting, as a mishap could upset the cart, rice porridge and all. I tried it and found that I was not equal to the task. She did not mind the hardship and our unequal cooperation went on swimmingly. All of us would go back for lunch at noontime. After a long rest, we would work again until dark and often were the last ones to have dinner.

I couldn't remember how many days we labored on that well until it finally reached the three-meter mark. When digging a well, the workers have to immerse themselves in water. This is usually done in wintertime when the water in the well is warm. But this was summertime and the water was icy cold. Ah-hsiang and I were afraid that the people who were working in the water might get sick on account of the chill. But they were so enthusiastic that they insisted they didn't feel cold at all. Unwilling to show womanly over-concern, the two of us made frequent inspections of the site and kept counsel to ourselves.

The water gradually reached the diggers' knees, thighs and then waists. Having attained a depth of over three meters, the well was now sufficient for irrigation use. I suggested that we celebrate by drinking *shaohsing* liquor which, incidentally, was an excellent preventive for colds. Everyone was delighted at the suggestion. One of the guest workers, the head of the logistics company, told us a strategy for obtaining liquor. I went back to the company headquarters and explained to the person in charge of the kitchen about our need, and borrowed a liquor bottle from him. He was an ingenious man. For fear that people would steal his liquor, he had a label with the word "Poison" and three exclamation marks pasted on the bottle. As if that wasn't enough, he had painted the picture of a skull and crossbones beneath it. There was some liquor in the bottle, about one inch, at the bottom. Hugging the dreadful bottle, I dashed to the "Center" which was located about two *li* west of the vegetable garden. All the way I was afraid that the cooperative at the "Center" might have closed its doors, because it was rather late in the afternoon, so I ran as fast as I could. However, having no certificate to buy liquor, I had to resort to diplomacy and the borrowed bottle to swindle the contraband. Miraculously, I succeeded. But what could we eat with the liquor? There was nothing except the pebble-like "fruit candies" of which I also bought a catty; and then I hurried back to the construction site.

Having finished digging the irrigation well, both stout and not-so-stout workers sat on the ground to recuperate. We shared the liquor by passing around various sized drinking cups with great zest. The bottle was quickly emptied except for one inch of liquor at the bottom which was returned to the kitchen. We also ate up all the fruit candies I had bought. Thus we celebrated the success of our venture.

I had no way of knowing how exhausted these hard workers were. I only knew my roommate, a woman colleague, who often cried "Ah yo" in her sleep as she tossed around. I was a light sleeper, and when I heard her groaning like this, I knew she must be dog tired. That increased my feelings of guilt. Once I heard some young men complain, "We're getting old." Apparently, they regretted that they were not as strong as they were in their twenties and that they could not do as much as they had wished.

The well we had dug now contained water almost to the brim. We bought a water-drawing contraption which was set up over the center of the well. A long shaft was attached to it. One had to push the shaft around to draw water. The longer the shaft, the bigger the circle one would have to travel. Walking in big circles was less likely to induce dizziness than walking in small circles. Some young people could make scores of rounds—some even over a hundred—without complaining of dizziness. Occasional visitors to the vegetable garden recognized that although crouching in the fields was strenuous, pushing the shaft was not easy either.

I followed my colleagues to the fields in the morning and came back at dusk everyday, doing light and insignificant things which did not properly deserve the dignity of being called labor. But since I was a member of the team, I felt that I had contributed something to its effort. Gradually, a sense of collective identity or group consciousness developed. Members of my team always identified ourselves as "us." A sentiment which, for lack of a better term, might be called the "us feeling" emerged. Generally speaking, when short-term collective labor is performed, workers disperse as soon as the project is completed. Such sentiment does not then develop. Intellectual workers can seldom work together collectively. When they do, each of them claims individual credit. When a group of intellectual workers are asked to undertake a collective project, those who do the research and those who do the writing can never get together and often work at cross purposes. But now that we were confined in the cadre school with no prospect of further development in sight, an "us feeling" had emerged as a result.

I heard my colleagues at the cadre school frequently complain, "After all, they have not been drenched by rain and scorched by the sun." The people they referred to belonged to the "them" group. Although we did not have the same background—some came from the "cow-shed" or the detention center for dissidents, and some from other sources—we all had the same collective mentality. Right or wrong, we were all under "their" control. But the demarcation line between "us" and "them" was very elusive. Not all those who controlled us belonged to the "them" group, neither did all of those "not drenched by rain and scorched by the sun." One leading cadre who flaunted his authority brazenly and whose lectures were studded with exclamations of "um" and "ah" was a typical member of the "them" group. In addition, individuals such as one nicknamed "shameless sycophant" and "self-styled national treasure" also properly belonged to that group. The gap between "us" and "them" was not a class difference. From my personal experience of collective labor, I learned a great deal about human nature and achieved a greater understanding of "class sentiment."

Our designated teachers, the middle and poor peasants, however, were not very obliging in their attitude toward the students of the cadre school. They stole one night the potatoes we had planted and harvested our vegetables as soon as they were ripe, saying, "You eat vegetables bought at the market. Why plant them?" The tree saplings we cultivated were stolen and sold at the market. When we were harvesting our soybeans, they came to our fields and helped themselves, saying, "You people eat commercial grains anyway." Perhaps in their eyes we too belonged to a "them" group, and were no different from those whose trademarks were "clothed in tatters but well-fed—each one with a big watch on his wrist."

Chapter 3

Leisure Between Chores at the Vegetable Garden

Every member of our unit worked hard and consumed a great deal of food. Could it be that we were following the maxim of "from each according to his ability and to each according to his need?" But this did not explain the whole story, for not everyone was paid the same amount of salary. For instance, I ate very little. Besides, I was physically weak, and was therefore assigned less strenuous work. Yet my salary was higher than average. Should I say I enjoyed unwarranted benefits from the "superior system of socialism?" To put it bluntly, I exploited the infinite bounty of the state for which I felt ashamed. But nobody seemed to take my mortification seriously. I therefore resigned myself to the study of the art of vegetable raising with complete devotion.

Starting a new vegetable garden involves a great deal of preparatory work, among which the building of a latrine is of the utmost importance. We selected a site bordering the main thoroughfare, in the hope that passers-by would favour us with their patronage and thereby increase our storage of fertilizer. Five posts were erected, one at each of the four corners and an additional one on one side to serve as a doorpost for our latrine. All we had to do to finish our work was to put up walls of kaoliang-stalk wattle on each of four sides, move in a big urn for receiving urine, dig two shallow pits as feces receptacles and place a few bricks around them as standing platforms. The only thing missing was a hanging curtain over the door. Ah-hsiang and I held a conference to devise a way to manufacture a hanging curtain. We painstakingly peeled the sheaths off some kaoliang stalks until the soft pith appeared.. Then we used fine hemp cordage to tie it all up into a handsome hanging curtain. With great satisfaction and pride, we hung the curtain at the entrance to the latrine which was distinguished by this unusual utilitarian decoration. But who would have suspected it—when we arrived at the vegetable garden the next morning we found that the hanging curtain had disappeared. Even the little accumulation of night soil had been stolen. From then on, Ah-hsiang and I took turns acting as a hanging curtain for each other when the call of nature prompted us to visit the latrine.

There were no fences around the vegetable gardens. Three other gardens belonging to the cadre school were situated to the west, south and southwest of our garden. One of them had a *deluxe* latrine whose pit was lined with solid bricks. By some ingenious devise the night soil poured automatically into an outside receptacle. But the night soil there was stolen as soon as it was accumulated. The local people believed that the excretions of the cadre school students were more fertile than those of the peasants.

We built a huge rectangular green compost pit, piling it up with the grass we had harvested. But as soon as we filled it, the contents were stolen, presumably to feed someone's cow. To the local people, even grass was a scarce commodity. We even saw people digging up dried grass roots to be used for fuel.

The units sent down earlier had built shelters of three to five rooms each on grounds adjacent to their vegetable gardens. We also hastily built a shelter to the southwest of the irrigation well. We put up a few posts for pillars and a wall of tamped earth on the north side of the structure. The wall was made of crumbly yellow loess earth mixed with clay and straw and pounded solid between wooden planks. The other three sides were covered with kaoliang-stalk wattles. A layer of kaoliang stalks and a piece of oilcloth covered the roof and a sheet of plastic was added underneath for extra protection. From a brick kiln situated in the northwest corner of the cadre school we carted two wheelbarrows full of broken bricks and spread them on the ground of the shelter. This was designed to reduce the dampness of the ground so as to render the shelter more habitable. A solid wooden door, complete with a working lock, was added to the structure. Three members of the vegetable team—the leader, the one nicknamed "Pastoral Poet,"and "Little Bull" lived there. We too used it occasionally as a resting place.

We planted the vegetable garden with all kinds of seeds, mostly green cabbage and turnips. In addition, celery-cabbage, chive, mustard green, lettuce, carrots, parsley and garlic seeds were also sown. All the newly constructed buildings, with the exception of those built by units sent down earlier, were concentrated in the vicinity of the Cadre School Center which was quite far from our vegetable garden. A plot of land near the new buildings was assigned to us for starting a new vegetable garden. Youthful and stout members of our unit were sent there to prepare the ground and to dig irrigation ditches, thus leaving the old plot unattended. Ah-hsiang and I therefore were ordered to take care of the old one.

Working on cabbage plants requires infinite patience. We rolled back one by one the curled leaves that did not cling to the head and tied them together with vines. Some plants grew satisfactorily, although the leaves did not cling together as tightly as they should. Ah-hsiang would carry over two half-full buckets of urine on a shoulder pole and I would scoop up the stinky fluid cup by cup to fertilize the plants. We had a special affection for a few turnip plants belonging to the "ivory" and *T'ai-hu* varieties which supposedly would yield long and white roots. When they emerged about one inch above the ground approximately the size of small rice bowls, we decided to cultivate them with special care. We even heaped the grass ash on them which the leader of our team had told us to use only in the radish field. But the turnips turned out to be an utter disappointment.

Fully anticipating that the roots would be at least a foot

long, I mustered all my strength to pull one out from the ground. Alas, I had misapplied my strength and unceremoniously fell on my back. The hidden root consisted of a few strands of miserable rhizomes; there was no succulent "meat" as we had expected. A more satisfactory yield came from the radish plants which were comparable to small pears in size.

When the weather turned cold, crouching in the field to weed and loosen the soil was a tedious job. The piercing north wind hit my back through my loosely-fitted jacket. We often did not go back for dinner until after dark. In December, our new building was completed and the whole company moved to the Cadre School Center. Ah-hsiang was assigned to work in the new vegetable garden. Only the three members who slept in the shelter continued to use it as their sleeping quarters. In the daytime, I was the only one who was assigned to watch over the old vegetable garden.

The assignment of watching over the old vegetable plot was a special favour accorded me by the leader of the team. Meh-ts'un's dormitory was very close to the brick kiln, about ten minutes walk from the vegetable garden. Meh-ts'un was the custodian of the farming implements of his company. The head of the team often ordered me to borrow tools from him. As borrowed things must be returned, I was thus enabled to see him not only once but twice on each assignment. I performed this chore with great enthusiasm. Meh-ts'un's job consisted of keeping track of the implements and performing occasional night watchman's duty by turn with others. His principal assignment was serving as messenger boy for his company. Every afternoon, he went to the Mailing and Telegraphic Office to collect mail, newspapers, and packages for distribution. The Mailing and Telegraphic Office was situated to the southeast of the vegetable garden. Meh-ts'un came by everyday alongside the little creek to the east of us and turned south toward his destination. Sometimes, he would make a detour to visit us. We welcomed this opportunity to talk and relax a little, but he would not dare to dally too long for fear of disrupting our work. When Ah-hsiang and I were working together in the field, she would suddenly tap my shoulder and say, "Look who is coming!" Meh-ts'un, with an armful of packages, would come toward us and the three of us would talk to each other across the creek. Later on, when I was watching over the vegetable garden alone, we discovered that the water in the little creek was so shallow that he could jump over without difficulty. From then on we would often meet in the vegetable garden, feeling as if we were re-enacting the romantic scenes of young lovers meeting clandestinely in rear gardens depicted so vividly in Chinese classical novels.

Meh-ts'un later found out that he didn't have to jump over the creek, as further south there was a stone bridge that he could cross. Every afternoon I would see him approaching slowly from the north of the kiln step by step with a hesitating gait. When the weather was fine, the two of us would sit on the bank of the irrigation ditch to enjoy the warm sun for a few moments. On days when he was late, he would only say a few words without sitting down and then hurry on his way. What he had to say was often irrelevant and incoherent, so sometimes he would put his thoughts on a piece of paper and have it delivered to me in person. Occasionally, I would lock the door of the shelter and walk with him a short distance beside the little creek. Then I would hurry back to my vegetable garden, watching the sight of his back disappearing gradually from my view. Oftentimes when he returned from the Mailing and Telegraphic Office with an armful of mail and packages, he would not come to my side of the creek to see me. We would exchange a few words of simple greeting across the water and return to our respective posts.

To me the vegetable garden was the center of the universe. There was a big earthen hill to the southwest which was known to the cadre school students as "Mount Fierce Tiger."[9] In the opposite direction in the northwest corner was the brick kiln. Further north of the kiln was Meh-ts'un's dormitory. The Cadre School Center was situated to the west of Mount Fierce Tiger. On the slope of the hill was the cafeteria of a certain company from which I bought my noon and evening meals. There were stoves in the shelters of the vegetable gardens to the west and to the south of us from which I often begged for boiled water. Since ours was an open stove constructed with three bricks, it was often difficult to light a fire when the wind turned gusty. Further south was the Mailing and Telegraphic Office which Meh-ts'un visited everyday. To the east of the creek lay a vast span of cultivated fields, stretching out as far as one's vision could reach. On the horizon there were a few green spots which were the villages of local peasants. Yang Village in which I once stayed when I first arrived, was further down to the east of these green spots. My daily activity was centered around the vegetable garden. I fancied myself as a spider sitting in the middle of a web that reached out in all directions. Coming into my web were bits of irrelevant information and thoughts which brightened, in some measure, my lackluster existence.

After breakfast every morning, I would tread back to my vegetable garden. On the way I would meet the three people who lived in the shelter walking toward the Cadre School Center for their breakfast. Arriving at the shelter, I would fumble for the key which was hidden in the kaoliang stalks piled beside the door. After putting down my eating para-phernalia—rice bowls, spoons and the like—I would lock up and start my daily routine of making rounds of the garden. The soil was rough and poor in the east end of the garden where radishes were planted and the produce left much to be desired. The bigger ones were often yanked out by people whenever I turned my back. They would pull the plants out in such a hurry that the broken parts remained visible on the surface. I would then dig them up and clean them with well water, which I could consume whenever I felt thirsty.

Green cabbage was planted in the field bordering the thoroughfare in the north. As soon as the cabbages were full grown, they were harvested by uninvited guests. Only their roots were left, showing that they had been newly cut. Once I discovered three or four heads of full-grown cabbage, lying scattered in the field. Apparently, whoever tried to steal them hadn't time to pick them up. From then on, we made a point to harvest the cabbages before they were fully grown. Once when I went to the back of the shelter, I saw three women pulling out our celery-cabbage. They ran as soon as they saw me. I gave chase, right on their heels. They threw their loot onto the ground as they ran, thinking that they would not be found guilty if they were caught without it. Actually, giving chase was my mandated duty. I would have preferred to let them take the cabbage home and make a decent meal out of it than to pick the cabbage up as it served us little practical purpose.

As a matter of fact, they were just passing by and the act of theft was spontaneous and accidental. There were often groups of people of ten or more, dressed in tatters of various shades coming out from the villages, who roamed the vicinity for the purpose of picking wild vegetables and collecting twigs or grass roots for fuel. They were often boys and girls from seven or eight to twelve or thirteen years old, led by a girl in her late teens or an older woman in her forties or fifties. Each of them was armed with a basket on one arm and a knife or a spade in the hand. They spread out in groups of two or three, searching for anything of value, ostensibly wild vegetables, to fill their baskets. They also cut down branches of trees in the nursery, hiding them in bundles at secret spots beside the road or creek. The loot was then taken away before lunch or dinner time. Some more daring youngsters even cut down tree saplings we planted and carried them away in huge bundles.

The kaoliang stalks piling up around the shelter were cleaned up by them. Three out of five posts which we erected over the latrine were stolen. Later, even the remaining two disappeared. The kaoliang-stalk wattles around the latrine and the shelter would be their next targets for sure. I had to wait until all the groups went away with their loot before I dared to go to Mount Fierce Tiger to buy my meals.

Once I witnessed the cabbage harvest of a neighboring vegetable garden to the south of us. They had a large number of workers who were strong and efficient. In comparison, our work lagged far behind, since most members of our team were old and weak. We spent a whole day cutting, digging, pulling, weighing, stock-taking and finally loading the cabbage unto a truck to be taken to the kitchen of the

Cadre School Center. The field was littered with discarded old, dried leaves. Before sundown, we sent the harvest away and cleaned up the field. An old woman and a young girl had been sitting in front of our shelter waiting to collect the discarded leaves. From time to time, the girl came to the field to assess the progress of the harvest and then went back to report to the old woman. Finally, the old woman stood up and said, "Let's go."

"They've cleaned up everything," said the little girl. "Even the landlords let us glean discarded leaves," said the old woman indignantly. I did not fully understand their local dialect. The only words I could make out were "feeding the pigs."

I asked the little girl, "What were you going to do with the old leaves?"

The girl replied, "If you bring a pot of water to a boil, then break the leaves into pieces and throw them in and mix them with wheat gluten, it tastes wonderful."

I often noticed that their "steamed bread" was of a reddish brown color, the same color of the wheat gluten. But I never knew how wonderful it could taste. We often complained about the tastelessness of the tough cabbage and bitter turnips which constituted our daily fare. The wonderful flavor of wheat gluten was something we should have experienced but had missed.

We planted some Chinese beets the yield of which was disappointing. The bigger ones were as large as medium-sized peaches and the smaller ones were the size of apricots. I was picking the edible ones from a huge pile, ready for the kitchen. The old woman watched me intensely and asked how they could be eaten. I said that they could be eaten either salted or boiled. I told her, "I'll keep the big ones and you may have the small ones." But she was very swift with her fingers in selecting the big ones to fill her basket, and I did not argue with her. Perfunctorily I took back a few big ones in exchange for smaller ones. She did not protest and went away happily. Later, I found out that they did not use the beets in the kitchen. I regretted that I had taken the big ones from her, but I was not authorized to give away our produce and it was not wise to establish a precedent. Once, as I was weeding in the vegetable garden, two young girls from the village came to visit me. I carried on a conversation with them by imitating their native dialect, albeit imperfectly. I gave them some surplus young seedlings and they in return helped me in the weeding. They referred to their menfolk as "big daddies." Their marriages were arranged by their parents; even girls as young as twelve or thirteen were promised in future marriages. One girl pointed a finger at the other one, saying, "She has been engaged and is expecting to be married soon." Embarrassed, the latter retaliated and said, "She has been promised in marriage to a family too." Both were illiterate.

The family with which I stayed when I first arrived was comparatively well-to-do. Two boys about ten years old were attending school, as there was no need for them to herd cows for a little extra income. However, their sister, about seventeen or eighteen years old, was illiterate. She had been engaged to a soldier of the Liberation Army from a neighboring village through a marriage broker at the insistence of her parents. The couple had never met. The young man had sent his fiancée a letter and a photograph of himself. From the photograph, he looked like a person of solid peasant stock and had received a primary school education. The girl's parents happened to share the same surname with us so I was addressed as "cousin." It therefore became the "cousin's" duty to write a reply to the future son-in-law. I held the pen for a long time without putting down a single appropriate word. Finally, the people who shared the dwelling with me made their contributions—one sentence here and another sentence there. The letter was thus haphazardly patched together. But the soldier was not favored with a picture of his fiancée.

Surprisingly, young men of fifteen or sixteen from the villages didn't seem to have regular work to do. They spent much of their time in small groups loitering around. With big baskets hanging on their backs, they searched for kindling

here and there. Occasionally they pulled up trees of considerable size and beat the ground with them, yelling in
unison, "Ha . . . Ha . . . Ha . . ." in order to scare up wild
jack rabbits. Once, three or four youngsters rushed into my
vegetable garden, yelling at the top of their lungs, "A cat!
. . . a cat!" In their dialect, cat and rabbit were synonymous.
I went out to have a look and told them there was no cat
in the vegetable garden. But the rabbit hiding there knew
that he had been detected and rushed out like a flash of
lightning. Several dogs pursued him relentlessly at the com-
mand of their masters and soon he was surrounded. In a
desperate effort to escape, the rabbit jumped six or seven
feet into the air, but when he landed, he was caught by the
dogs. My heart ached for this unfortunate creature. From
then on, when I heard "Ha . . . Ha . . . Ha . . .," I knew
what was going on and refused to look further.

On one occasion on January 3, 1970, to be exact, at
approximately three o'clock in the afternoon, several strangers
arrived and, pointing at two earthen mounds located to the
southeast of the vegetable garden, asked me if they were
the grave sites of the cadre school. There had been several
tractor drivers who had come with the first arrivals to the
cadre school and one of them had been drowned in the
river when his tractor overturned on the bridge. The strangers
wanted to know whether one of the mounds was the grave
of the deceased driver. I told them that it was not and that
he was buried in a grave way over there, pointing at a mound
at a distance. After a little while, I saw several people shoveling
dirt beside the creek to the east of our turnip field. A truck
was parked there. The contents of the truck were covered
with a straw mat. "Ah!" I said to myself. "They are burying
somebody." Several uniformed soldiers stood beside the truck.
They probably belonged to an Army Propaganda Unit.

I saw three or four people shoveling; their movements
were very swift. One person jumped into the pit, followed
by another and then a third. A soldier walked toward me;
I thought that he probably wanted some water to drink. But

in fact, he wished to borrow a shovel, because one of theirs had broken. I took one from the shelter and gave it to him.

There was no villager in sight. Only a few diggers working hastily and quickly. After a little while, only their heads and shoulders were visible. The pit had attained sufficient depth. From under the straw mat, they brought out a corpse in a blue uniform. I was a little startled and witnessed the burial at a distance.

When the soldier came to return the shovel, I asked him whether the deceased was a man or a woman and what ailment he had died of. He said that the deceased, a male, aged thirty-three, had belonged to a certain company and that he had committed suicide.

In wintertime days were short. When the truck left the burial site, a veil of desolation permeated the evening atmosphere. There was no other person in the vegetable garden. I walked slowly toward the burial site. Only a new, rather flat mound was visible. No one would notice this new grave beside the creek.

The next day I told Meh-ts'un about the incident. I advised him to be careful not to step on the new mound, because there was no coffin and the body was only a few feet underneath the surface. When he came back from the Mailing and Telegraphic Office, he was full of information about the deceased. Not only was he informed of the man's name, but he also knew that the deceased had a wife and sons and that several pieces of his baggage had been sent to his home.

A heavy snow descended a few days later. I was afraid that the weight of the snow might cause the newly filled mound to cave in allowing homeless dogs to drag out the corpse. But fortunately, there was no crack in the mound; only it became a little flatter than before.

I was the sole custodian of the vegetable garden throughout the winter. As soon as the sun appeared in the eastern horizon amidst multi-colored clouds, groups of villagers from near and afar, old and young, clad in tatters of various shades would converge in the vicinity of the vegetable garden, collecting whatever salvageable articles they could. They would not leave until sundown. Only then would they depart in small groups with their baskets full of collectables. I would buy my evening meal after they left and return to the vegetable garden, consuming the food slowly in front of the shelter. The rosy light of sunset would disappear gradually and the evening mist would descend on the vegetable garden. Soon it would be pitch dark, and there would not be a single soul around, not even a visible lamplight in the vicinity. I would enter the shelter where numerous rats frolicked in the piles of kaoliang stalks, making strange noises. Then after washing my bowl and spoons with well water, I would lock up and return to the dormitory.

Everyone was busy doing his or her assigned work, while I alone enjoyed leisure. I felt ashamed of myself, as well as being bored of my meaningless existence. Although I was not as active as the "Instructor of the Imperial Guards of 800,000 Strong," I was not as desperate as the monk Lu Chih-shen in the novel *Water Margin,* who was confined in a monastery in Mount Wu-t'ai.[10] I shared his feeling toward the cloistered life.

While I was lodging with a peasant family, I did not work at the same place as my housemates. So I could not go back to the house in their company. Often I walked back alone and enjoyed the solitude. I preferred to walk in darkness. With a flashlight in hand, I could only see a small circle around me, not knowing where I was. But somehow I was able to find the tortuous way home around the surrounding clustered rocks and desolate mounds. When I approached the village, I could see at a distance the lamplight flickering beyond the trees. There was my place—a narrow bed, covered with a mosquito net. It was not my home; it was only a lonely resting place. I recalled a picture of an old man, carrying a bag and a walking cane, straggling slowly on a winding road on a slope toward his grave. Was my lot any different from that of the old man in that picture?

After the turn of the year, at the "bright and clear" festival time, the Research Department's cadre school moved to Ming-kang. Before departure time, the whole vegetable team returned to dismantle all constructions on the site. Anything that could be pulled down or taken apart was removed. A tractor ploughed the field over. Meh-ts'un and I had our last glimpse of the place. The shelter was gone, the structure over the well dismantled, the irrigation ditch levelled, and the vegetable garden ploughed under by the tractor. Even the flattened earth mound had disappeared. What remained was a span of flat land strewn with solid clods of dirt.

Chapter 4

Love for a Cute Little Dog

The "Pastoral Poet" of our team once brought back a yellow puppy from the brick kiln. The poet's name was Ch'ü, a homonym of the word meaning "run." In a spirit of playfulness, Ah-hsiang named the puppy "Hsiao-ch'ü" or "Little Ch'ü, the Runner" in honor of the poet. To retaliate, the poet wanted to name the dog after Ah-hsiang. In his roundabout way he called her "Ah-ch'ü," thus making her share a part of Ah-hsiang's name. But "Hsiao-ch'ü" was easier to pronounce than "Ah-ch'ü," so the former appellation stuck. Few people outside the vegetable team knew that the dog had been named after the poet.

We built a doghouse to the south of the shelter for Little Runner by carefully arranging pieces of broken bricks and paving it with kaoliang stalks. Cold in winter, it was not a cozy retreat for a dog and the stalks did not make a comfortable bed. The vegetable garden was crisscrossed with irrigation ditches. Once I stepped into one and got my socks and shoes soaking wet. Although the weather was still warm, I had to endure the discomfort for a whole day. When Little Runner first arrived, she had the misfortune of falling into a ditch and plastering herself with wet mud. The chill made her shiver uncontrollably. We rubbed her with kaoliang stalks which were too stiff to be of any help, then put her in the sun to warm up. But the wintry sun, at best, was only lukewarm, while the breeze accompanying it had a chilling effect.

Little Runner had been born in a poor and desolate village in Honan. While she was with her mother, she could have a few drops of milk to sustain her life, whereas we had nothing to feed her with. All we could obtain from the kitchen were a few scraps of potato and bread crumbs. One venerable old gentleman of the vegetable team, always "correct" in his ideology, caught us feeding the dog with discarded crumbs from a white-flour bun. Incensed, he gave the leader of the team a thorough scolding. "Have you seen what the peasants are eating? And you are feeding the dog with white bread!" This instilled in us a deep sense of shame, and from then on we could only discreetly feed the dog with pieces of potato from our plates. Actually, neither potato nor bun was appropriate food for a dog. Little Runner was thin and weak and her growth was stunted.

One day, Ah-hsiang, looking embarrassed, whispered into my ear, "I have something to tell you." She was choked with laughter before she could continue. She said bashfully, "Little Runner, you know . . . steals human excrement for food . . . in the latrine . . . how disgusting!"

I couldn't control my amusement at her naïveté and said laughingly, "Look at the way you talk. I thought for a moment that you did it yourself."

Ah-hsiang, however, expressed her real concern. "What if she continued to do that as a habit? Wouldn't it be too filthy?" I told her that all dogs in the villages ate excrement. When my daughter was sent down to a village, she shared a brick bed with a baby girl. At first whenever the baby soiled the bed and mat with feces, my daughter would rush to clean it up with toilet paper. The woman of the house scolded her for wasting paper as well as the natural resource—excrement. She called, "Wu . . . lu, lu, lu," and a dog appeared who quickly lapped up the mess that was on the brick bed, the mat and the baby's buttocks as well. It was done efficiently, with no washing and no wiping. From then on, every morning when she heard her neighbors calling "Wu . . . lu, lu, lu," my daughter knew that her neighbors' babies were feeding their dogs.

Not until I came to the village did I understand why

people considered pigs filthy animals. Dogs and pigs shared the same gastronomic tastes. But pigs cared less about their table manners, and appeared more greedy and less considerate than dogs. A pig would push down a squatting man while he was performing his duty. A dog, however, would wait on the side patiently; when all was ready, the dog would wag its tail and enjoy its meal in a civilized manner. When I lived in the village, not only did I become acquainted with all the village dogs, but I also provided them with material for sustenance as well.

If pigs and dogs were considered filthy, I wondered, could we consider vegetables clean? Vegetarians, I thought, probably never knew what was used as fertilizer in raising vegetables.

I told Ah-hsiang that there were two old sayings describing the stubbornness of people who refuse to change after repeated admonitions and the difficulty in reforming one's nature. One was: "If you could change, dogs would not eat excrement anymore." The other was: "Your behavior is no different than that of a dog taking a vow of abstinence in front of a latrine." Little Runner was not a foreign dog—she had never tasted the canned dog food made in the West. She was also less fortunate than the dogs kept by other companies. I heard that members of other companies were allowed to feed their dogs with scraps from the kitchen. Their dogs, therefore, were robust and had glossy coats. The leftovers from our kitchen were used exclusively to feed the pigs, because the pigs helped us raise our production quotas. What Little Runner did was an instinctive reaction to insure her continued physical existence.

Whenever Meh-ts'un came to visit me, he would bring pieces of tough meat with bristles on them or bones with tendons still attached to feed Little Runner. Little Runner would express her welcome openly, jumping and frolicking. Once, he brought with him two rotten eggs someone had thrown away. "Pa, Pa!" Meh-ts'un tossed one after another at Little Runner who swallowed them voraciously, lapping up the spills; not even the shells were ignored. When I was watching over the vegetable garden alone, Little Runner would keep me company and wait for Meh-ts'un's arrival.

As soon as she saw Meh-ts'un at a distance coming toward us from the north of the kiln, she would meet him halfway, jumping up and down, barking and wagging her tail vigorously. As if these demonstrations were not sufficient to express her welcome, she would throw in a somersault. After the somersault, she would get up, wag her tail and jump up and down again, which would be followed by another somersault. Meh-ts'un, throughout his life, probably had never received such enthusiastic welcome from any living creature. Her antics prevented Meh-ts'un from proceeding until I shouted at her to make way for him. The three of us went back to the vegetable garden together.

A colleague of mine often bragged about his precious grandson. He said that whenever he returned home, his grandson, three years old, would welcome him by yelling and jumping; after that he would roll over on the floor. The proud grandfather gave out a hearty laugh each time he finished relating his story. I, too, had a weakness for children, but I did not dare to compare his grandson with Little Runner. This led me to ponder on a number of questions: Do dogs have human traits? Do humans sometimes exhibit dog behavior? Do children and puppies share any common characteristics?

Whenever Little Runner saw a familiar face, she would try to follow that person around. Before we moved to the Cadre School Center, whenever Ah-hsiang and I went to the company canteen for meals, Little Runner would follow us. She was only a little puppy then. The way she toddled along like a baby learning its first steps softened our hearts. We thought she might hurt herself, so we put her in the doghouse and blocked its door with a piece of brick before each trip. One evening, when we were already halfway to the company canteen, we discovered that Little Runner was following us stealthily. Apparently, she had broken out from the doghouse. It was a rainy day; the road was slippery. Despite our threats and scolding, she persisted in following us. She wobbled along until she reached the shelter which was our kitchen-cum-dining-room. Everyone present fell in love with her and saved a morsel from his or her own mouth to feed the puppy. Little Runner enjoyed a full meal and returned to the vegetable garden with the leader of the team. This was her first venture of a long journey.

When I was watching over the vegetable garden alone, I often went to Meh-ts'un's unit for meals. Knowing that Little Runner could not be confined in the doghouse, I locked her up in the shelter. Once when I was approaching the kiln, I found that Little Runner was following me discreetly at a distance. Apparently, she had loosened the wattle wall and gotten out. I tried to yell at her to halt. Little Runner stopped and looked at me quizzically. But as soon as I reached Meh-ts'un's dormitory, she was right on my heels. Overjoyed as soon as she saw Meh-ts'un, she bounced and jumped like crazy. His roommates all loved the cute little puppy and fed her with whatever they could spare. Once again Little Runner went away with a full stomach.

At first Little Runner was contented in welcoming Meh-ts'un to the vegetable garden. Later she would follow him along whenever he made an appearance, but she would stop at the creek and come back. One day Meh-ts'un discovered that she had followed him a long distance. Fearing that she might get too tired, Meh-ts'un caught her and brought her back to the vegetable garden. While I held on to her, Meh-ts'un slipped away. However, when he returned from the Mailing and Telegraphic Office, he was surprised to find that Little Runner had already reached his dormitory, and was barking and jumping to greet him. The welcoming ceremony over, she came back to the vegetable garden to keep me company.

After the whole company moved to the Cadre School Center, Little Runner survived on the little scraps that the leader of the team managed to bring back to the vegetable garden. This was rather inconvenient. Hence, she also moved to the Center where she could be fed with the leftovers from the kitchen, but this move made her lose contact with the vegetable garden. Although I went back to the dormitory every evening, I never knew where she spent her nights. Since there were plenty of people who deemed that keeping dogs as pets was an indulgence of ladies of leisure in capitalist society, I restrained myself from showing undue affection for her. But somehow Little Runner discovered the room where I stayed in the dormitory. On several occasions when I went back, my roommates would say, "Your Little Runner has come several times to look for you." I often brought back some scraps such as pieces of bone to feed her to express my appreciation. When I left for the vegetable garden every morning, she would try to follow me, only to be stopped by my loud scolding. One time I even threw a pebble at her. She stopped and gave me a forlorn look from a distance. Once on a drizzling day when I was languishing in the shelter alone, I heard a sound: "Woof!" There appeared Little Runner, wagging her tail and barking vigorously. After a little while she sat beside me contentedly. Apparently, she had found the way from the Center to the vegetable garden.

If I went to Meh-ts'un's unit to have a meal, it would take at least half an hour to cover the distance plus the time for eating. The vegetable garden could not be left unattended for so long. I therefore often bought food from the canteen of a certain unit on the slope of Mount Fierce Tiger which could be reached in six or seven minutes. Everytime Little Runner came to visit me, I would buy a full portion of food and share it with her. Although the distance I had to travel was not far, the wind on the road was pretty cold. I often cupped the bowl with both hands to keep the rice and vegetables warm, but to no avail. I had to warm the food in my mouth before I slowly swallowed it. Little Runner, however, was impatient; she would jump up and down, demanding to be fed immediately. I would hold the bowl up high with one hand and shovel a spoonful of food into my mouth and then another into a piece of paper for her with the other hand. Without such maneuvering, my bowl and spoon would not be spared from her licking. Thus we would delightfully share our meal. After that I would wash my bowl and spoon, put things together, and bring Little Runner back to the Center.

Little Runner could not give me any protection. Instead, I had to protect her, because in the short span of three months she had grown from a puppy to a "junior miss" dog.

There were building materials such as lumber and sundry matters piling up on Mount Fierce Tiger. A ferocious dog called Tiger and a nameless grey mongrel, no less ferocious, were kept there to guard the materials. Both expressed their admiration for Little Runner, who, being pre-adolescent, was instinctively afraid of them. Each time we walked past them, I had to shout at the two huge animals, ordering them to desist. As we had to walk a long way beside the creek, I would walk on the embankment and she on the slope, hiding herself from the stare of the amorous creatures. She would not feel safe until we crossed the bridge and reached the other side.

Luckily I knew these two dogs, because I had purposefully made friends with them. Once I was late in finishing my evening meal and it was pitch dark when I reached the west side main road after locking up the shelter. Suddenly I heard "Woof . . . Woof . . . Woof," and was confronted with two luminous eyes. I could see the outline of a huge black dog, with his back hunched and a hideous look on his face. That was Tiger, the most ferocious dog of the cadre school. I remembered that when I lived in the village, each time I had gotten lost on the way back in the night, all the dogs of the village would bark like mad and surround me in a circle if I made a hesitating move. On such an occasion, I would shout at the top of my voice, "Dogs!" imitating the familiar tone of the villagers. I was told that the village dogs were not given individual names. They would retreat peacefully. When Tiger appeared suddenly in front of me, I was quite frightened. Out of habit, I stood still and shouted "Tiger!" He didn't jump on me, but only cried "Woof, woof," and sniffed at my feet docilely. From then on, whenever I met Tiger on the road, I always called his name and fed him with something. I didn't know the name of his companion, the grey dog. But I always gave them a friendly greeting. For I had not forgotten what I had been told as a child: never show that you are afraid of a dog! Apparently I had not revealed to them my inner weakness and utter vulnerability.

After we moved to the Center, we were required to perform

rotating night patrols. Methods of conducting night patrol differed from one company to the other. In our company, the patrols were divided into four shifts, with each shift lasting two hours.

The first shift was from ten o'clock to twelve at night and the last shift was from four to six in the morning. These two shifts were assigned to the elderly and weak as a special consideration, since staying up late or rising early were better than interrupting one's sleep in the middle of the night. Each patrol was manned by two persons, except the first shift which consisted of one person. It was said that the first shift was comparatively safe, since incidences of burglary often happened between three or four o'clock in the morning. Few opted for the first shift which was patrolled by a single person. I volunteered for it because I loved to sleep late and no one was competing for the job. Donning an enormous long fur overcoat which belonged to the office and armed with a flashlight, I performed patrol duty alone after the ten o'clock lights-out time. The area covered by the patrol was quite large; one would start from the main road in the north, reach the cadre school public ground used for showing cinema pictures and return by the road around the new vegetable garden and the pigsty. Ten minutes after lights-out time, there was absolute silence in the area. Time passed slowly as I walked in the darkness. Sometimes I was not alone, for Little Runner would accompany me for a few rounds and break the silence with her familiar yelp. This reminded me of the cat, Little Calico, who accompanied me home every night during the "Three Anti-Movement" period at Tsing-hua University.[11] By nature I was a timid soul. Whether there were ghosts or not, I was afraid of them all the same. Even in brightly lighted places, not to speak of complete darkness, I could be frightened easily by unspecified causes, preventing me from walking from a room in the east wing to a room in the west wing. However, I underwent a complete transformation during the "Three-Anti" period: I was no longer afraid of ghosts of any kind. Meetings of our section often lasted until eleven or twelve o'clock at night. I walked home alone from the northwest corner of the university campus to the dormitory in the southeast. There were several places on the way of which I was particularly afraid. When I passed by these places alone in the daytime or in the company of others at dusk, I often felt the jitters. But during the "Three-Anti" movement, I was not afraid of anything anymore. At that time, Meh-ts'un had been assigned temporarily to work in the city; Ah-yüan lived in school, and our domestic helper had already gone to sleep. Only Little Calico waited for me in the bushes for my return. Like Little Runner, she would utter a "meow" and rush toward my feet. With her front paws, she would embrace my leg loosely. If I were still as timid as before, I would have been scared out of my wits. After that she would dash ten feet ahead of me and come back to welcome me again, jumping back and forth until we reached the door. She would then look up to me while I fumbled for my key and opened the door. Little Runner reminded me of many anecdotes connected with Little Calico. We lost her when we moved to a new dwelling and never kept a cat again. If I had achieved an understanding of the Buddhist precept of "never sleep under a mulberry tree for three nights consecutively," I would never have lavished my love on a homeless dog like I did. But Little Runner seemed to have insisted that I was her master— perhaps the feeling was mutual; I couldn't give her up.

Once a colleague in our company went to Hsing-tsai by bicycle and Little Runner followed him all the way. The colleague, also a dog lover, bought a bowl of noodles for Little Runner. On the return journey she got a free ride in the basket attached to the bicycle. But Little Runner was sick with exhaustion, and lay there motionless and noiseless. Everyone thought she was going to die. When I went back from the vegetable garden, someone told me: "Your Little Runner is dying. Why don't you go and have a look?" I followed him quickly. As soon as I called out, "Little Runner," she recognized my voice, jumped up, yelped a few times and wagged her tail nonstop. That relieved everyone's anxiety. They said, "Great! Great! Little Runner will live." I wondered why Little Runner's well-being had suddenly become the concern of so many people.

At New Year's, the kitchen worker bought a dog to cook for food, because dog meat was cheaper than pork. Some villagers loved dogs and wouldn't sell them to people for food, while others would sell them, but couldn't bear to kill them; still others would have them killed for sale. The one our kitchen bought had been killed by its owner. According to some northerners, dog meat had to be cooked over a hardwood fire until it was *al dente*. Then it should be eaten with chopped scallions—could this have been Lu Chih-shen's way of eating dog meat?[12] Following the suggestion of Ah-hsiang, the cook red-braised the meat with a liberal dose of soypaste and heavy oil, together with plenty of scallions and ginger. When I went to the canteen to eat that night, I bought a portion of the red-braised dog meat for myself and others to have a taste. The meat was tender, not too lean and not different from fatless pork. Many people said that Little Runner wouldn't eat dog meat, raw or cooked. According to our "Pastoral Poet," Little Runner once had carried a piece of the dog meat in her mouth and buried it in a hole that she had dug with her front paws. I didn't believe the poet and asked him repeatedly about the accuracy of his statement. He asserted definitely that he had seen Little Runner burying the meat with his own eyes. However, I still think that the story was one of the poet's beautiful inventions.

News of the impending move of the cadre school came one day suddenly. The leadership told us that all dogs belonging to the different companies were to be left behind. There had been a detachment of the Liberation Army stationed in the Center before we moved. Ah-hsiang and I brought Little Runner over and introduced her to the soldiers. We told them we couldn't bring her along, and implored them to take care of her. One soldier said, "Don't worry. We'll feed her. Many of us love little animals." We told him that the little dog's name was Little Runner so that they would know how to call her.

On moving day, things were so chaotic that no one seemed to have seen Little Runner. She probably was on an outing with her friends. After we moved to Ming-kang, someone went back to the Center to attend to some unfinished business. He told us what he heard from the people over there: "Your little dog refused to eat and ran back and forth, yelping all the time as if she was searching for someone." Could it be that Little Runner was searching for me? For Meh-ts'un? For those in our company who had paid any attention to her? We regretted that we hadn't disobeyed orders and brought her to Ming-kang, as some people from other companies had done with their pets. But those dogs brought to Ming-kang were finally expelled too.

Whenever Meh-ts'un and I reminisced about the little dog we would say, "Wonder what happened to Little Runner?"

Meh-ts'un would answer, "Maybe she has been eaten and turned into a pile of shit."

I would say, "She'd be better off eaten. Perhaps she has become an old bitch, and survives on human excrement, raising litters of puppies, one after another. . . ."

Chapter 5

Lucky Breaks
in Several Escapades

Anyone who had attended the cadre school in Hsi-hsien would never forget the rain there—it was a relentless, grey torrent that seemed to engulf all of humanity, turning the road into a complete quagmire. Even the floors inside buildings were soaking wet as if they were about to be transformed into sheets of mud. Although the edges of the ruts on the road, having been baked by the hot sun, could be as sharp as knives and could cause blisters on our soles, as soon as it rained, the road would quickly become a sheet of slippery mud. Even with the help of a walking stick, one could not avoid slipping and falling. When we were billeted with peasant families, some of us frequently fell, turning into veritable mud pies when we went to the canteen for meals. The canteen was composed of two connecting mat-sheds. A third shed was used to store carts and tools. At mealtimes, with our bowls in our hands, we squeezed under the two mat-sheds. The centers of the sheds were comparatively dry. However, those who stood on the periphery not only would get their feet soiled with mud, but would also be pelted by raindrops that came in with the wind. But no matter whether one stood in the center or on the periphery of the shed, one could not avoid the drops of water that came down from the top. After taking our meals, we would slide our way to the well to wash our bowls. If, unfortunately, anyone

broke a thermos bottle accidentally on his way back to the
village, it was truly an irreversible misfortune. For a thermos
bottle could not be bought locally; neither would it be
practical to order a replacement by mail from Peking. Alas,
the rainy days of Hsi-hsien were truly catastrophic.

Once it rained incessantly for several days. By that time,
we held study sessions in the village only in the mornings.
The leadership and the core personnel, however, continued
to hold meetings in the afternoons. The rest of us were free
to do anything we liked. Many went back to their dwellings
to write letters, mend clothes, or prepare winter garments.
I lived with the family of an assistant group leader. Although
the house was only a little one with mud walls on all sides,
it was comparatively more elegant than the other dwellings.
A hole of a window, about one foot in width and half a foot
in height, was carved into the wall facing south. We pasted
a piece of oiled paper over it, making it wind proof and
translucent. My bed was located in a draftless, dark corner
of the room. It was so dark that when I held out my hand
I could not see all my five fingers. The room was tolerable
to sleep in at night, but it was impossible to stay there in
daytime. I would not appropriate the dimly lighted little
space under the window for myself. In addition, changing
my rain gear—raincoat, waterproof pants and high rainboots—back and forth was a bother, as was finding a place
to hang the dripping umbrella, so I decided to brave the
rain on one occasion, with an umbrella in one hand and a
walking cane in the other.

When I lived in my hometown, Soochow, I loved rainy
days more than anything else. The trees and bushes in the
rear garden wore a new coat of intense green after the rain
and the pebbles that paved the streets were washed clean
of any residual dust. It would give me the feeling that I,
too, had been cleansed both bodily and spiritually. But the
rain of Hsi-hsien only reminded one that man was truly
made of dust and that one's body, bones and all, would one
day turn into mud. As I walked out of the village in the
rain into a sea of mud, I looked at my watch and realized
that it was only a few minutes past two o'clock. A sudden

thought came to my mind: "Why not pay Meh-ts'un a surprise visit?" I knew that leaving without permission was against the regulations. But I was sure that there would be no bugle blowing, falling into ranks, and roll-call at this time. So I decided to sneak around the kitchen to reach the westbound main road.

All the connecting fields had irrigation ditches which were dry most of the time. But after the rain, the accumulated water turned them into streams of all sizes. As I went across a little bridge, I found that the road connecting to it had been inundated. The water in confluence with that of the ditches had formed a small river. I did not want to turn back, because it was only a few steps away from the main road. I tested the shallow water near the bank gingerly. Despite a few deep spots, I was able to negotiate the slope without incident. Looking backward, as I saw no one was on my heels, I headed west on the main road, while making a mental note that I would avoid this place when I came back.

The road was so slippery that I had to walk slowly, one step at a time. My rainboots became heavier with each step. Every now and then, I had to stop and scrape off the mud from the boots with my walking stick. My rainboots were quite high, but so much wet mud stuck on them that they had become "rubber bouncers"[13] which had a constant tendency to fall off from my feet. On several occasions I almost left them in the mud. In addition, several clods of unknown origin mysteriously found their way inside my boots. When I walked on the south side of the road, I thought it would be less slippery on the north side because there was more grass there. But as soon as I moved to the north side, the south side looked more grassy. The road was a level and straight thoroughfare, but there had been a cave-in on the road foundation about twenty to thirty feet in length near the brick kiln. When we were digging the irrigation well, Ah-hsiang and I often pushed the meal cart to the vegetable garden passing through this stretch of road. It was always Ah-hsiang who pushed the cart up and down the slopes. As it had rained for several days consecutively, this place had become a big pool with clear water covering the shallow bottom. It looked as if there were two embankments visible under the water. But as soon as I stepped on one, my foot quickly sank deep into the mud. The embankments were only mud ridges made by a heavy cart, which, soaked with water, had turned into "spongy embankments."[14] Since I had already covered such a long distance with some difficulty, even though some of the road had been flat and level, I would not turn back at this point. Besides, the water did not reach the top of my boots, and was still about an inch or two short. The bottom of the pool was covered by sand or grass. Both the sandy and grassy places had firm as well as soft spots. Using my walking stick to probe before taking each step, I miraculously forded the big pool safely and without incident.

After I climbed the slope and reached the brick kiln, I should have turned north. A little stream running from north to south poured its water into a low lying wasteland to the west of the kiln, after swirling a little at the foot of the slope. Normally the stream rambled along at the bottom of the wasteland, but the rain had swelled it into a swift current, leaving a tiny island in the middle. I followed the river bank and walked north, but the span of the water became wider and wider. Meh-ts'un's dormitory, the last of several rows of grey tiled buildings, was on the other side of the river. I figured that the width of the river at this point was at least ten feet. A little bridge of four or five feet in width which used to span the river had been washed away by the flood and was now floating haphazardly downstream. The incessant rain seemed to have united the sky and earth together into a solid whole. It occurred to me that this formidable river with its ten-foot span had unceremoniously and completely cut off my road. Looking toward the east side of the river from where I stood, I could see Meh-ts'un's room which was at the westernmost end of a row comprising over a dozen rooms. But not a single person was in sight then. Suddenly I thought that if I were detected standing there alone I would become everybody's laughing stock. There was nothing that I could do except turn back, negotiating my every step on the difficult muddy road. I planned my course of action while I walked. It seemed that the further south the river flowed, the narrower its span became, and the swifter its current ran. If I went all the way back to the slope beneath the brick kiln and jumped over onto the little island and then onto the shore, wouldn't I be on the other side of the river? But, as I could see, the other side was strewn with rocks of irregular sizes and small pebbles, without a single path leading anywhere. On the other hand, as long as the land was continuous and not interrupted by rivers or streams, I should be able to reach my destination. The mud on the river bank was extremely slippery and wearing rain-boots as I did made me less surefooted than if I had had my cloth shoes on. Again, I wasn't sure if the ground of the little island was firm enough to support my weight. When I reached that spot, I extended my walking stick to test the ground and found it quite firm. By sticking my walking stick deep into the earth, I vaulted myself over onto the island, and by repeating the process several times, I put myself on the other side of the river. I slushed through the torturous path with one foot in mud and the other in the water, step by step, and after suffering numerous hardships, finally managed to reach the door of Meh-ts'un's dormitory.

I pushed the door open, determined to give Meh-ts'un a pleasant surprise.

"How did you get here?" he exclaimed. Laughingly, I said, "I came to see you."

He was so exasperated that he ordered me to leave immediately. I didn't dare dilly-dally too long either, because after consulting my watch I realized that it had taken me twice as long to get there as it would have taken under ordinary conditions. I was also afraid that the little island might get smaller as the water swelled and that I might not be able to go across the river. And if the grey sky turned darker, I might sink into the muddy pool if I attempted to cross it.

By chance a member of Meh-ts'un's unit had to go to the Center on some official business. He intended to go by the brick kiln and turn west. I told him that the flood had washed away the bridge, but he said it didn't matter, as there was another way further south. I decided to follow him. Meh-ts'un put on his rainboots, brought an umbrella and accompaneid us for part of the journey. After we reached the brick kiln, the man turned west while I headed east. The rest of the way was what I had just travelled a little while ago. Knowing that all I needed to do was to exercise a little patience and caution, I proceeded with added boldness. It was pitch dark when I reached the kitchen. Dinner time was over, but there were still lights on in the shed and I heard voices there. Like a thief, I stealthily passed by the kitchen. Hastening my steps, I let my muddy feet carry me back to my room.

I couldn't recall what I had for dinner that night: half a bun I had saved? Something Meh-ts'un had given me? Or perhaps nothing at all. I congratulated myself for not having fallen into the river, not having gotten stuck in the quagmire, not having slipped in the mud and not having been caught by the leadership. Even my roommates hadn't detected the unusual activity I had indulged myself in.

Another adventure took place in the wintertime after the whole company had moved into the new building we had constructed for ourselves. The Army Propaganda Unit had decided to give us a joyful holiday by providing us with a lavish new year's eve dinner, assuming that it would lessen our homesickness.

The foreign language section to which I belonged was originally a part of the literature section. The "old men" of several female workers in my section worked in the literature section. (Meh-ts'un was my "old man." All husbands were called "old men" regardless of their age.) We agreed to invite these "old men" to share the new year's eve dinner with us. The cooks in the kitchen vied with each other to show off the excellence of their culinary art. Many delectable foods were prepared including such popular dishes as smoked fish, duck cooked in bean paste, red-braised pork, curry beef and many more. In addition, there were salads which were also very tasty. Meh-ts'un gladly joined the vegetable team group and, sitting around a rectangular table, we enjoyed an epicurean feast. Little Runner ate her fill under the table and wagged her tail so hard that I was afraid it might fall off.

I remembered that on Meh-ts'un's sixtieth birthday, by way of celebration, we had opened a can of red-braised chicken. Incidentally, my sixtieth birthday by Chinese reckoning was not far away, so we celebrated both together. That day happened to be a day off for me, but not for him. Usually we had two meals on our days off and three on ordinary days. I had gone to Meh-ts'un's place after I had my breakfast and did not feel hungry at noon time. As I couldn't stay for dinner before I was due back, I had had only a few bites of a bun that evening. Now, at the new year's eve feast, we had been supplied with delicious food as well as fine wine. Although both of us were teetotalers, we had a good time with the others on this joyful occasion and forgot all our worries. After dinner I accompanied Meh-ts'un on his journey back to the dormitory. We talked on the way until we reached the bridge where a tractor had overturned. Meh-ts'un turned to me and said, "You'd better go back." He went across the bridge and headed north; this was only the half-way point of his journey.

There had been a heavy snow the day before. The accumulated snow on the main road had melted somewhat and mixed with dry dirt. When we treaded on it, it felt soft underfoot, neither slippery nor hard. But on the paths north of the bridge the snow had not melted, and it was getting dark. I was afraid that Meh-ts'un, being near-sighted, could not find his way home—he had never had a good sense of direction anyway—so I decided to accompany him all the way.

Under the snow, roads and fields became indistinguishable, as they were covered by a continuous span of white. I tried to take mental notes on all the special features at various spots; for instance, how many trees of different sizes there were at a certain turn of the road, what were the shapes of these trees, at which spot of the road was there a bend, at what place the snow was unusually thick, where there was a snow covered ditch with half melted mud underneath that should be avoided on my return journey. Meh-ts'un's dormitory was brightly lit when we arrived. As it was late, I did not dare to linger and started to leave. A young man in the room said, "It's already dark. Let me bring you home." I thought that since this was new year's eve when everyone was having a good time, laughing and talking in a warm room, it would be an unreasonable imposition on him to bring me back on such a cold night. So I said it was unnecessary since I knew the way well. However, Meh-ts'un became apprehensive, so I boasted, "There's not a single day that I haven't travelled on this road twice! Besides, I have a powerful flashlight. There's nothing to be afraid of." Actually, the roads I had used were the embankment on the south side and the east-west thoroughfare on the north side. Meh-ts'un was unaware of the fact that in a short span of half an hour the sky outside had completely changed and that the road was no longer in the same condition as when we had travelled on it before. Neither had I realized that although it was easy to find the road when one travelled from darkness toward a brightly lit building, that travelling from a lighted place into darkness was a different story. As I resolutely declined the offer of the young man to bring me home, he did not insist. Meh-ts'un walked me as far as the light reached, then I told him to turn back.

I was proud of my experience of walking in the dark. I stood still to orient myself. Someone had said that most women comrades had no sense of direction. A certain book, I remembered, indicated that women and hens were the only two creatures that would lose their bearings as soon as they left their homes. This was probably a deliberate insult on womanhood. But I, for one, was an animal with no sense of direction at all. I often found myself in a situation depicted so correctly by an ancient poet: "Wanting to go to the south city, I ended up in the north."[15] Despite Meh-ts'un's poor sense of direction, I had always depended upon him to find our way. Now I had to figure out the directions for my journey back alone. I decided I would head for the southwest first and then cut through the wooded area diagonally until I reached the main thoroughfare beside the woods; then I'd proceed toward the west, looking for the spot where three or five trees stood; from there I'd turn to the south, go across the bridge and reach the main road leading directly to my dormitory.

But alas, as soon as I stepped beyond the circle reached by the light, I was surrounded by a mass of complete darkness. There was no star visible in the sky, and a layer of white snow covered the ground. I could see neither trees nor paths. When I turned on the flashlight, all I could see were tree branches, some near and others at a distance. Turning off the flashlight, I let my eyes get accustomed to the darkness. When I opened my eyes again, I saw nothing but a massive chunk of darkness around me and a layer of white snow on the ground. I remembered that when we had passed this place at dusk, we could barely discern the winding path in the woods by the weak light emanating from the dormitory. Now, there was absolutely nothing that could be seen. I almost turned back to beg for an escort. But a second thought told me that with the snow covering the ground even an additional pair of eyes would not be of much help. Furthermore the person who brought me home would have to come back by himself. I'd rather brave it myself alone.

I was sure that I hadn't made a single move while I was contemplating. Now, I had to plunge into the darkness and head roughly toward the southwest. However, if I veered too much to the west, I'd never come out of the woods. I'd better veer to the south, I decided. The ground appeared to be smooth and white. But as I stepped on it, I discovered a sea of mud underneath. Fortunately, the mud was mixed with kaoliang stalks, broken twines and fallen leaves, so the ground was not too slippery. I took care to walk toward the south. Whenever my path was blocked by a tree, I moved to the west a little to bypass it. Turning my head, I could no longer see the light of Meh-ts'un's dormitory. I had lost my bearings completely. Walking on, I suddenly stepped onto a soft spot and fell into a ditch. This scared the wits out of me. But instinctively I remembered that there was a deep, wide ditch along the main road. Could this be it? I was almost glad that I had fallen into it. Quickly I turned on the flashlight and found a way to climb up the slope and onto the main road beside the woods.

On the main road there was no snow which made travelling easy. I walked briskly in long strides. I figured that I had to turn south at an appropriate point. If I kept on walking straight ahead, I would reach the neighboring village west of the Cadre School Center. There were trees lining both sides of the road, at intervals of a dozen or so paces. But I could see only their trunks, not their branches or leaves. Neither could I discern their shapes. The landmarks that I had tried to remember so hard earlier had completely eluded me. My only concern was that if I missed the turning point I would not be able to find the bridge from which the tractor had fallen. It would be better for me to turn sooner rather than later, for if I turned too late, I'd stumble into an expanse of continuous fields in which I might spend the whole night going in circles. So when I saw a cluster of trees in one spot, I turned south immediately.

But as soon as I left the main road, I lost my bearings again. After a few steps, I found myself in the midst of a kaoliang field. I continued to forge forward, for as long as I was walking toward the south, I'd reach the river, and so long as I could reach the river, I'd find the bridge sooner or later.

I often heard people say that kaoliang fields were hiding places for criminals in dark nights. I was also afraid that village dogs would come to attack me when they heard the noise I was making. So I listened closely to surrounding noises and moved along silently without disturbing the dried leaves on the kaoliang stalks. The ground was muddy, but not too slippery. I made full use of my five senses to feel my way around in complete darkness, without the benefit of the flashlight. I was unaware of the distance I had thus covered until I came upon a road with a high embankment behind it. I had reached the river at last! However, in the snowy, dark night, the familiar road had changed completely and I couldn't make out whether I was on the east side or the west side of the bridge—for there was a high embankment on the west bank of the river too. If I were on the west side, it would be necessary to reach another brick kiln west of the Cadre School Center before I could cross the river, since the further west the river ran, the wider it became. From there I'd have to turn east in order to reach my dormitory. I had heard that a student of the cadre school had committed suicide by hanging himself in the brick kiln. Fortunately, I wasn't as easily scared as I had been in earlier days. Otherwise, knowing that someone had drowned under the bridge and another had hanged himself in the kiln, I'd be scared to death there. I figured that in my impatience, I had turned too soon and that I was still on the east side of the bridge. I veered toward the west and after a while found the bridge.

After crossing the bridge, although I had only reached the halfway point, I covered the remaining distance with unusual speed and soon arrived at the dormitory.

"You're back already?" My roommates greeted me with friendly smiles, as if I had been out just for a leisurely stroll. In the brightly lit room, no one could imagine that an entirely different world could have existed in the dark wilderness outside.

In the spring of 1971 all members of the Research Department moved from Hsi-shien to a military division barracks in Ming-kang. The curriculum of the cadre school also was changed from performing physical labor to conducting "study sessions"—sessions designed to study class struggle, no doubt! There were people who didn't understand why our institution was called "Research Department;" now they were suddenly enlightened—the Research Department was in reality a "Study Department."

Movie viewing was considered part of our study, and no one was allowed to play truant. (Meh-ts'un, however, was excused because of his bad eyesight.) On a night when a movie had been scheduled after dinner, we would bring our collapsible stools, fall in line and march to the square. Each company had its designated location. We would put down our stools in their proper places in neat formations. When it rained in the morning or afternoon, if the designated location had turned into a quagmire, we had to put our stools in the mud. Sometimes we had to bring our rain gear when there was the prospect of rain. On hot nights no preventive measures could be taken against attacks of large swarms of mosquitoes. But movie viewing sessions entailed no examinations. I could open my eyes to watch and close my eyes to rest anytime as I wished. There were only a few old movies anyway; whatever I missed while resting my eyes could be seen in the next round. After returning to the dormitory my thirty-odd roommates would discuss the plot, but I kept my mouth shut so as not to reveal my ignorance.

Once after a movie viewing session, everyone began to march back to their dormitories as usual. I was still day-dreaming, my eyes fixed on the heels of the people in front of me. Gradually the ranks up front dispersed and I found myself in a corridor of a dormitory which was not my own. I quickly rejoined another group of which only a few last sections remained. Soon they too disappeared into their dormitories. I didn't know where my dormitory was located. I asked several people; no one seemed to know. As they were in a hurry to go back to their rooms, they didn't want to be bothered. Like a person in a strange place without any friends or acquaintances, I felt depressed and lonely.

Looking up, I saw that the sky was full of stars. I could recognize a few of them, but it seemed to me that they were not in their right positions. I had not learned how to determine directions by looking at stars, but I knew enough to realize that I was far away from the dormitory, just because the stars I knew were not in their usual positions. The campsite occupied a wide, open space which was littered with numerous barracks, all brightly lit at that moment. The area was also crisscrossed by numerous paths and all the barracks were of the same style. If I spent too much time wandering around, I'd be unable to find my dormitory before the lights-off time. There was only one way, I figured:. to find the stone-paved main road running around the south boundary of the campsite and then find my dormitory. The square in which the movies were shown was close to the main road and, in my estimation, so was the strange dormitory that I had stumbled into a little while ago. Most of the barracks were facing south and the Great Dipper was behind them—this much I knew. All I should do was walk away from these barracks toward the south to find the main road. Even if it were a roundabout way, it would be easy walking.

As I didn't want to waste time by following the zigzagging paths, I went straight toward the south by taking shortcuts and ended up in a vegetable garden of the campsite. This was quite different from the vegetable garden we had kept in Hsi-hsien. The soil here was fertile and the plots were covered with vegetables so luxuriant that they made the boundaries between beds indistinguishable. I was aware of the fact that there was a feces receptacle between every two beds of vegetables. These receptacles were very deep. Not long before this, one young, tall fellow of our company had fallen into one after a movie viewing session. He had climbed out and gone to the "water closet"—our wash room—and scrubbed and washed himself for a long time in spite of the cold weather. He had gone back to his room quietly so that the incident was not over publicized. If I should have stepped into the receptacle, I would have sunk right to the bottom and my cries for help would have invoked no response. As to the prospect of suffering the horror of taking a cold bath, it would not have been worth considering at all.

I had not changed the batteries of my flashlight, because I thought that I would be following the ranks and that the flashlight would not be needed. Now my flashlight gave out a feeble light which enabled me to see only the leaves of vegetables of unknown varieties. I thought that I could imitate the way "Pigsy"[16] had walked across a frozen river. But unlike "Pigsy" I did not have a carrying pole to keep my balance. All I could use was a collapsible stool. But if I were to fall into a receptacle even only up to my waist, I would eventually sink to the bottom if immediate help was not forthcoming. It then dawned on me that I shouldn't permit myself to indulge in such idle notions. Armed with the stool in one hand and the flashlight in the other, I walked slowly and gingerly through the vegetable garden, kicking aside every leaf on the way. Even though I was very anxious to get home, I took every step with utmost caution as if I were walking beside a deep abyss. With much difficulty I finally got myself out of the garden, but after crossing an irrigation ditch, I found myself in yet another vegetable plot. It was a genuine nightmare. I kept on walking and walking—I thought I'd never leave the garden.

Fortunately, I was walking in the right direction, and finally I left the vegetable garden. After stepping over a path paved with coal cinders, a cluster of weeds and a pile of stones, I finally reached the stone paved main road. I covered a length of the road at top speed, running and walking alternately. Then I turned north and ran directly to my dormitory. The lights in the dormitory were still on. The last group of women who had gone to the lavatory had just come back which proved that the time I had spent in the vegetable garden had been less than twenty minutes. Therefore, I had not wasted too much time in taking those wrong turns. It appeared as if I had just come back from the lavatory. Who would have imagined that I had followed the wrong group with my eyes wide open? If I had had the misfortune of falling into one of those receptacles, I wondered when I would have been discovered.

As I laid my tired body down on the hard, solid little bed, I enjoyed a sense of unusual relief and comfort.

A comrade two years my junior had been sitting peacefully on her collapsible stool, watching the movie one day after dinner. When the show was over, she had suffered a paralyzing stroke. All first aid efforts proved to be of no avail and she died as a result. From then on old folks were excused from attending the movie sessions. If I had yelled in front of the strange dormitory for help that night, I wondered, would they have decided sooner to free old folks from attending movies? My predicament, however, might not have been considered as tragic enough; maybe it could only have been used as a negative lesson.

To me, the three incidents mentioned above had been adventures. But actually they could not really be properly classified as such, because all adventures involve the element of danger. In the absence of danger, my "adventures" could only be considered as foolish escapades.

Chapter 6

Rumor Versus Reality

When I was living in Wu Village, my landlady's cat once played a nasty trick on me. Every night we kept an oil lamp burning on the wall near the door. My bed was located at the farthest corner of the room, and was always enclosed in a dark shadow. One night, my roommates and I went to the well to wash up before turning in. Upon return, we discovered two strange looking piles on my bed. Luckily, we didn't try to remove them with our hands. Turning on my flashlight, I found a dead mouse with its abdomen wide open, its body smeared with blood. Beside it, there was a pile of pinkish innards. Neither of us dared to pick them up. Nervously, I removed my pillow and comforter. My colleague and I picked up the four corners of the sheet and dumped the dead mouse into the compost pile in the yard. The next morning I got up early to wash the sheet using one bucket of well water after another. After it had dried out under the sun, I washed it again. But the blood stain somehow refused to go away.

When I met Meh-ts'un I told him of the unpleasant incident, saying that the cat had treated me with a dead mouse. Meh-ts'un tried to comfort me by saying, "This is an auspicious omen. Maybe you'll leave here soon. The body and the innards of a dead mouse were separated and put in two piles. That signifies 'separation.' The word 'separation' is a homonym of the word 'leave.' The word for mouse is a homonym for the word 'place.' It is obvious that you'll soon leave this place." This invoked a hearty laugh from me. No matter how well-meaning and clever his methods were, which ranged from dream interpretation to word analysis[17]—all traditional ways of fortune-telling—I remained unconvinced. I should have shouted at him in the style of the "big-character poster" writers: "It is quite clear what kind of ideological background you were reared with! Thinking of leaving here? Not a chance!" Truthfully, despite his pleasing words, we both knew the maxim, "Freedom is the acceptance of discipline." Knowing perfectly well that when a door is securely shut, ramming and pushing it is of no avail.

Toward the end of the year on one of his visits to the vegetable garden, Meh-ts'un informed me of an extraordinary rumor. While visiting the Postal and Telegraphic Office daily on official business, Meh-ts'un had frequently helped the workers there to recognize difficult words and to locate obscure place names. He was highly regarded by these workers for solving their problems and was often entertained by them with tea receptions. The so-called tea reception, however, was usually nothing more elaborate than a cup of boiled water. But what Meh-ts'un enjoyed was real tea, with leaves steeped in boiling water. One of the comrades revealed a guarded secret to him—a telegram from Peking to the cadre school had ordered the return of those students belonging to the "old, weak, infirm and disabled" group; the list of returnees contained Meh-ts'un's name.

I was overjoyed. I figured that if Meh-ts'un could return to Peking, he would be able to live with Ah-yüan, making life more tolerable, and that even though I had to remain in the cadre school, I'd be less worried about them. Besides, I could go to Peking on my annual leave to visit them. At that time, the workers of the cadre school in Hsi-hsien did not enjoy this privilege, even though they and their spouses did not live together.

After a few days, Meh-ts'un made a special effort to see me on his return trip from the Postal and Telegraphic Office, informing me that the list of the "old, weak, infirm and disabled" returnees had indeed arrived and that his name was on it.

I even made plans to pack his things for him and waited anxiously for the date of departure. A few days later, he came to see me, with his usual calm expression on his face.

"Has the list been made public?" I inquired.

"It has been made public, but I am not on it," he said. Then he told me the names of those who were leaving for Peking.

My heart sank as he recited the names of the lucky ones. If there had been no rumor, there would have been no false hope, no disappointment, and no frustration.

I walked with him to the river bank and then returned to the shed. While watching his back gradually disappear from view, I was troubled by a thousand unsettling thoughts. Was Meh-ts'un any younger or more vigorous than the others? I recited to myself a poem by Han Yü entitled, "Written for Secretary Chang on the Night of August Fifteenth"[18] which invoked a deep sentimental response in me.

The first thought that came to my mind concerned the "black material" in Meh-ts'un's dossier, the existence of which would never have come to our attention if not for the glorious Great Cultural Revolution.

In the early stages of the Great Cultural Revolution, some people jointly attacked Meh-ts'un in big character posters, accusing him of taking a contemptuous attitude toward the writings of the leadership. Those who knew Meh-ts'un only slightly said after seeing the damning material: "That guy Ch'ien would have put it more sardonically if he had said something to that effect. This doesn't sound like him at all." Someone informed me of the attack. I was furious when I saw the poster. I said, "If someone wanted to chase the wind and catch the shadows, there should be at least a trace of wind and a ghost of a shadow, but there is none. No one should be allowed to frame others without any plausible grounds." As soon as Meh-ts'un and I returned from our respective "cowsheds," I immediately told him of the false accusation. Together we drafted a small character poster, outlining every possible lead to the false accusation and demanding a thorough investigation. After dinner, we hurriedly went to the Research Department, bringing with us a bottle of paste and a flashlight, and secured the small character poster directly underneath its accusing predecessor. The next day, I became the object of a serious struggle on account of this. However, later we found that what had been written in the big character poster was not entirely groundless. Someone had, indeed, denounced "a certain fellow Ch'ien" for having uttered such-and-such disloyal words. Apparently, this accusation had been put in the file of Meh-ts'un's dossier without verification. When the actual investigation was carried out, the accuser denied he had ever made such an accusation. Presumably, the investigation conducted by the Red Guards was thorough, and they found no evidence to sustain the accusation. Before Meh-ts'un was sent down to the cadre school, the Army Propaganda Unit thought that the accusation was serious in nature and that although the investigation had found no evidence, there were some grounds for suspicion. Meh-ts'un, therefore, was ordered to write an essay of self-criticism. Meh-ts'un had to handle the matter in a tactful way and handed in an essay full of ambiguous statements. Whenever I thought of this incident, my chest felt full of indignation.

Meh-ts'un came to the vegetable garden one day and I said to him, "It must have been the black material in your dossier that caused all the trouble." He thought this was sheer nonsense, for the list had been officially announced, so it didn't matter what had caused the trouble. I admitted that I was being unreasonable, for indulging in wishful thinking was silly and refusing to forget old scores was even sillier.

On the day of departure of the people who had been permitted to go back to Peking, we all got up early and went to the main road around the square to give them a send-off. Sending others home while staying behind put me in a peculiar mood. I watched one big truck after another, fully loaded with people and baggage, leaving the cadre school. This scene aroused in me mixed emotions. Suddenly a woman colleague grabbed my arm and said, "Let's go back!" Together we returned to our dormitory. She gave out a long sigh and looked as if she wanted to say something, but stopped. Silently we went to our respective rooms.

Those returnees had belonged to the "sick, weak, infirm and disabled" group. Now that they had been sent back, we who remained had to resign ourselves to our fate, anticipating that we would have to stay in the cadre school for the rest of our lives. I went to the vegetable garden alone where an idea came to my mind: If I had sent Meh-ts'un back to Peking, would I have been able to preserve that sense of solidarity with the members of the group whom we called "us"? I was afraid that despite my physical presence in the cadre school, my emotional state would have been altered and I could have no longer considered myself a full member of the "us" group. My mind went back to the days just before Liberation when so many people were scrambling for a chance to leave the country. Why didn't we take the chance when several had been offered? Had it been due to our progressive ideology? Or our high political consciousness? By way of rationalization, Meh-ts'un often recited two lines from one of Liu Yung's poems: "I've no regrets if my girdle becomes loosely fit; / For her, suffering haggardness, I mind not a bit."[19]

We simply could not forsake the motherland. We could not bear to leave "her," which included the collective "us." Although we had no personal contacts with the millions of people whom we called "us," every single one was a component of the whole. We shared the same lot and were closely connected with one another. Each component was inseparable from the other. Now I felt ashamed of myself for being led by a false rumor and entertaining such absurd wishful thinking. What I had hoped—that Meh-ts'un would be able to go back to Peking to be close to Ah-yüan—showed that I cared only for the welfare of my own family and nothing else. Since the Liberation, after undergoing countless reforms, one after another, I had become a worse person, I was afraid, than I had been before.

On one of Meh-ts'un's visits, I pointed at the shed and said: "Give us such a shed and we'll settle down here. Would that be all right with you?"

After several soul-searching moments he replied, "There are no books."

It was true that all material comforts could be dispensed with, but it would be very boring without a few books around. In Meh-ts'un's trunk, there were still a few dictionaries, miscellaneous notebooks and stone rubbings.

"Do you regret that you chose to stay at that time when you had a chance to leave?" I asked.

"Even if I could turn back the clock, I would do the same thing," he replied.

It was in his nature to often make quick decisions, as if no deliberation was necessary. Once he made a decision, however, he never regretted it. I was the one who always hesitated when facing a problem, but we inevitably came to the same decision. Since we had made the choice with our eyes widely open, we accepted our fate and indulged in no more fancy illusions.

After the cadre school moved to Ming-kang, my dormitory and Meh-ts'un's were separated only by a row of buildings. The distance between the two could be covered on foot in five to six minutes. Our dormitory was a tiled building, with glass windows and concrete floors. The food there was better than that served in the canteens of the Research Department. The latrine was less primitive with no stalk wattles or shallow pits and we didn't have to line up to use the facility. Our living quarters were spacious and we could freely use our reference books and notebooks that we had brought with us. From Peking Ah-yüan frequently mailed us not only foodstuffs but foreign language newspapers and magazines as well. Books circulated underground among friends were read over and over. The environment of the dormitory was pleasant and quiet enough and there were plenty of spots worth lingering in. The two of us often took strolls together at dusk—a definite improvement over our meetings in the vegetable garden. As we performed neither physical labor nor mental chores, we were ashamed of ourselves for being paid without lifting a finger. But after seeing a large group of promising young men and women doing nothing except conducting meetings and making speeches, we could not help but secretly worry about the future of the country.

The students of the cadre school actually had nothing to do, but no one was allowed to leave. The railway station was only an hour away by foot, but without a written permit from the Army Propaganda Unit, no ticket could be bought. One day Meh-ts'un had a toothache and I eye trouble. We managed to obtain simultaneous sick leaves for the purpose of visiting the medical center in Hsin-yang. The hospital there had just introduced an innovative technique of "tooth extraction by massage"—supposedly a simple and painless procedure. But no one dared to try it, and all prospective patients had disappeared. Meh-ts'un and I, instead of visiting the clinic, went to visit a scenic spot the name of which we have since forgotten. The so-called "mountain" was only an earth mound; the "lake" only a half-dried pool. There was also a dilapidated bridge and a few patches of vegetable seedlings lodged in a hollow ground. Although there wasn't much to look at, we felt happy because we had played truant for a day. Later, I went to Hsin-yang alone to have my eye examined. It was discovered that there was a lesion in my tear duct, but my request for sick leave to be treated in Peking was flatly denied by the Army Propaganda Unit. I had to ask for a personal leave which required the approval of the Research Department before I was permitted to register at a hospital. This strict rule was probably made to prevent students of the cadre school from leaving for Peking to seek treatment and not returning.

Anyone in the cadre school with a serious illness had to entrust his life to luck. Upon the completion of the treatment for my eye in Peking, I brought Ah-yüan with me to the cadre school for a family visit. When we arrived at Ming-kang, fully expecting Meh-ts'un to be at the railway station waiting for us, we couldn't find him either on the platform, nor on the road to the cadre school. We were afraid that we might have missed him at the railway station. I was unaware of the fact that he had become seriously ill—an attack of bronchial asthma with high fever—soon after I left for Peking. Ah-yüan and I learned of this from someone in

the vicinity of his dormitory. The health worker of his
company was not even a barefoot doctor. According to her
own account, it was the first time in her life that she had
ever administered an intravenous injection. She was so ner-
vous that she broke out in a sweat all over her body and
forgot to loosen the rubber tourniquet on Meh-ts'un's arm
after the injection had been administered. But somehow, the
two injections proved to be effective. When Ah-yüan and I
arrived at the cadre school, his fever had subsided. The
health worker, pointing a finger at her own nose and turning
her head upward a little, said proudly, "Mr. Chi'en, you
know, I saved your life." What she did was indeed a feat.
Had she been afraid or refused to administer those two
injections, Meh-ts'un would have had to be transferred to a
distant hospital for treatment, the result of which could have
been disastrous.

After Ah-yüan's visit, our worries about each other lessened,
but the fact that everyone could fill his stomach while doing
nothing created a tense atmosphere. We learned from the
newspaper that Lin Piao had "caught a cold and bit the
dust." After that the struggle against the "May Sixteen" group
lost its punch. Even so, the "old, weak, infirm and disabled"
returnees to Peking were still busy holding meetings and
attending study sessions.

It is well said that a hope held ardently enough will be
realized sooner or later, but as soon as it is realized it is
not the same as envisioned. In March 1973 another batch
of "old, weak, infirm and disabled" people was destined to
go back to Peking, and both Meh-ts'un's name and mine
were on the list. This happened at a point when I had
almost given up all hope of returning. Now, my only prayer
was that all our colleagues could go home. But so long as
there was a second group, there would be a third and a
fourth. It looked as if all the students of the cadre school
would be sent back in groups sooner or later. I was secretly
glad that we were in the early group. Our friends felt happy
for us and gave us send-off parties. Since the stove in the
dormitory had not yet been dismantled, we cooked a few
dinners of rice dumplings and meat and escarole won-tons—

the escarole had been picked in the wild. These well-wishers were also away from home, but their mood was much more generous than mine when I had seen people off a year ago. I had a sense of guilt when I faced those whose names were not on the present list of the "sick, weak, infirm and disabled" group. But neither my guilt nor my gratitude toward the well-wishers could suppress the joy that I tried to keep in my heart. From this I came to realize something about myself: after undergoing more than ten years of reform, plus two years of training at the cadre school, not only had I failed to achieve the level of progress that everyone was striving for, I hadn't even been able to eliminate whatever selfishness that was in me. I was still my old self.[20]

It has been six years since I came back to Peking. Little incidents of the past are still fresh in my mind as if they had happened only yesterday. I have written these six chapters to record this period of my life which I consider to have been a valuable experience.

Notes

1. Meh-ts'un 默存 is the courtesy name of the author's husband Ch'ien Chung-shu 錢鍾書. Calling one's husband by his courtesy name was considered to be perpetuating a custom of feudal society which could have brought trouble to the writer.

2. The "Worker and Liberation Army Propaganda Unit" refers to the "Propaganda units of Mao Tse-tung thought" organized by activists in various factories and army units. They were separately called "Workers' propaganda units" and "Liberation Army propaganda units." During the later part of the Cultural Revolution, incidents of physical struggles and bloody fighting occurred in various universities and cultural organizations. Mao ordered the stationing of Liberation Army units in troubled areas to assist the workers' propaganda units. Intellectuals were forced to undergo re-education by the workers and soldiers as a means of changing their outlook on life.

3. Yü P'ing-po 俞平伯, born in 1899, a famous essayist and critic, was active in literary circles in the twenties and thirties. He was the grandson of an illustrious Ch'ing scholar Yü Yüeh 俞樾 and known as an authority on the famous Chinese novel, *Hung-lou-meng* 紅樓夢 or the *Dream of the Red Chamber*. In 1954, under the direction of China's cultural czar, Chou Yang 周揚, a campaign against Yü P'ing-po and Hu Shih 胡適, was launched for their failure in interpreting China's literary heritage in terms of class struggle. While admitting

his guilt, Yü argued that the author of *Hung-lou-meng* was innately anti-feudal and that the characters therein were essentially not politically conscious. Yü was permitted to continue his research as a member of the Chinese Academy of Sciences. (See Howard L. Boorman, *Biographical Dictionary of Republican China* New York: Columbia University Press, Vol. IV, 1971, pp. 67-70.)

4. The phrase "peculiar, melancholy sentiment of departure" is adapted from a famous lyric poem by Li Yü 李煜 (937–987), the "Last Emperor" of the Southern T'ang dynasty. While a captive in the capital of the newly founded Sung dynasty, Li wrote many sad and nostalgic poems which were suspected as having a subversive effect on the conquered populace. To remove the possible threat to the new regime, his captor, the Emperor T'ai-tsung of Sung, ordered his death by poisoning. The second half of the poem 剪不斷，理還亂， 是離愁，別是一番滋味在心頭。may be rendered as follows:

> Cut and cut, it severs not.
> Sort and sort, it remains a tangled lot.
> T'is the grief of departure, a peculiar,
> Melancholy sentiment, that sticks to my heart.

5. Ho Ch'i-fang 何其芳, born in 1910, was a leading figure in the Communist cultural hierarchy. He taught literature at the Lu Hsün Institute of Arts in Yenan and later became its director. After Mao Tse-tung's *Talks at the Yenan Literary Conference* in 1942, Ho and Chou Yang became the arbiters of the arts and literature and demanded strict conformity with the guidelines laid down by the Party. In 1954, Ho was deeply involved in the so-called "Hu Feng 胡風 affair" in which he was attacked as a blind worshipper of authority and a persecutor of young progressive writers. Ho launched a nation-wide counterattack on Hu Feng who was arrested and imprisoned in 1955. Despite his slavish adherence to the "correct" party line in art, Ho was sent down for re-education during the Cultural Revolution period. (See Howard Boorman, *op cit.* Vol. II, 1968, pp. 58–60.)

6. The 516 Group or May 16 Detachment was a splinter

group in the Red Guard Movement. It appeared first as an ultra-leftist group under the control of two radicals, Wang li 王立and Kuan Feng 關鋒 of the Central Cultural Revolutionary Committee. When its activities became too violent, involving attacks on veteran revolutionary old guards as well as a small group of leaders in the army, it was suppressed by the joint effort of Chou En-lai and Lin Piao. Mao was forced to declare it a counter-revolutionary organization and ordered a search for its backers. Tens of thousands of innocent youths were sacrificed in the process.

7. The expression *ai-jen* 愛人 or "lover" is the mainland term for spouse. Its origin can be traced to the Yenan days when the marriage ceremony was shunned as a part of the bourgeois or feudal tradition. Without the marriage ceremony, the terms "lover" and "spouse" became indistinguishable. The appellation should have been rendered obsolete when the marriage law was proclaimed in 1951. The expression, however, has persisted. It would be ironic, for instance, for an estranged couple to call each other lover in a divorce court. The word "lover" here does not involve any romantic or illicit implication, for Chinese Communist sexual morality deviates very little from the traditional Confucian standard. Only visitors from bourgeois societies find it embarrassing to call their spouses "lovers," perhaps a psychological hang-up derived from the dissipating sexual mores of the West.

8. During the Cultural Revolution period, Chiang Ch'ing ruled that "in all literary and dramatic works, there must be a few positive proletarian figures among all the characters; among all the positive proletarian figures, there must be at least one outstanding heroic figure." There was no outstanding heroic figure in the well-drilling skit. Therefore, it could be subject to criticism.

9. The reference is made to one of Chiang Ch'ing's eight model revolutionary operas, *Taking Mount Fierce Tiger by Strategy* 智取威武山. Famous retired Peking opera actors were ordered to play in it and the title of the opera became a household word.

10. Both Lin Ch'ung 林冲, the "Instructor of the Imperial Guards of 800,000 Strong" and Lu Chih-shen 魯智深, nicknamed

the "Intractable Monk," are two lovable characters in the classical novel *Water Margin*. The former is a serious, responsible and brave man, while the latter is an unorthodox, happy-go-lucky monk who does not abide by strict monastic regulations.

11. The "Three-Anti Movement" was carried out in 1952 with the purpose of eliminating "corruption, waste and bureaucratic tendencies in society." Innocent people were sometimes sacrificed as scapegoats, while real villains got promotions and reaped benefits.

12. The reference is made here again to Lu Chih-shen, the "Intractable Monk" in *Water Margin*. One amusing episode in the famous novel describes how the "Intractable Monk," in defiance of monastic rules, complains that his palate is being ruined by the lack of delicacies in his daily fare. He steals a leg of dog meat and gorges himself on it, while pouring countless goblets of wine down his throat.

13. The author uses a pun here by referring to her boots as *Chiao Li-shih* 膠力土 or "rubber bouncers". During the reign of Hsüan-tsung (r. 713–756) of the T'ang dynasty, when the famous poet Li Po was ordered to write poems in the imperial presence, a powerful eunuch by the name of Kao Li-shih 高力士 or "Kao, the Muscle Man" condescended to pull the boots off Li Po's feet and the famous beauty, Concubine Yang Kuei-fei, ground a stick of ink for him. The pronounciation of the words *Chiao Li-shih* 膠力土 is approximate to that of "Kao Li-shih" 高力士 .

14. This is an allusion to an embankment built by Su Tung-p'o 蘇東坡 (1037–1101) commonly known as "Su-T'i" 蘇堤 or "Su's Embankment" which has become a scenic spot in West Lake, Hangchow. The author calls the two ridges under water "spongy embankments" because the word *su* 酥 or "spongy" is a homonym for Su Tung-p'o's surname.

15. Here the author has unwittingly misquoted a word in a line of Tu Fu's 杜甫 (712–770) poem and twisted the meaning of the quotation completely. The original words are: 欲往城南望城北 or "I wish to go to the South City to gaze toward the North." She has mistakenly substituted the word *wang* 望, "to gaze," with the word *wang* 往, "to go." The two words are homo-

phonous, except that the former is pronounced in the fourth tone while the latter is in the third tone. The quotation is adopted from a poem called *Ai-chiang-t'ou* 哀江頭 or "Lamenting Beside the River" which was written in the spring of 757 A.D. The capital city Ch'ang-an had fallen into the hands of the rebel An Lu-shan 安祿山 in the previous year. The Emperor Hsüan-tsung had slipped out of the city in July of 756 on his westward journey to find refuge in Szechwan. While on the way, the Emperor's bodyguards mutinied and demanded the death of his favorite concubine Yang Kuei-fei who was finally strangled to placate the angry soldiers. In August, the crown prince set up court in Ling-wu, some four hundred miles northwest of Ch'ang-an, to fight against the rebels. Later he was known as the Emperor Su-tsung.

Tu Fu lived in the capital city occupied by the barbarian hordes for several months after the fall. In this poem, Tu Fu starts to describe what he sees on a spring day along the bank of a meandering river—the deserted palace with its doors and windows shuttered—and wonders who is there to enjoy the new greenery put forth by the willow trees and young rushes. The scene reminds him of the days gone by when the Emperor's procession would march toward the South Park. He recalls how the first lady of the palace would sit beside the sovereign in the imperial carriage. Maids of honor, riding on white horses with golden bits, would shoot passing birds with bows and arrows to amuse their lord and themselves. The poet laments that all this gaiety and merriment have now vanished, and that the blood-tainted wandering soul of the imperial lady cannot find its way back. In conclusion, he writes, "At dusk the city is covered with dust kicked up by the hooves of the barbarian horses. I wish to go to the South City to gaze toward the North." Historical records point out that the South Park was located on a hill. The poet wanted to go there in order to turn his eyes toward the North where the new court had just been established. (See David Hawkes, *A Little Primer of Tu Fu,* Oxford, the Clarendon Press, 1967, pp. 49–55.)

16. "Pigsy" is the Anglicized name for Chu Pa-chieh 猪八戒 in Arthur Waley's translation of the novel *Hsi-yu-chi* 西游記 or

Monkey. Pigsy is one of the three disciples of the monk
Tripitaka who embarked on a journey to the West to obtain
Buddhist scriptures. A comic and cowardly figure, Pigsy lacks
religious conviction and cannot resist the temptations of
gluttonous and sensual delights. He uses a nine-pronged
muckrake with a long handle as his weapon. The reference
of walking across a frozen lake is found in an episode in
which Pigsy advises his master to carry his staff crosswise,
saying, "Ice always has holes in it. If you put your foot in
a hole, down you go, and unless you're holding a stick
crosswise like this, you can't stop yourself." (See *Monkey*
by Wu Ch'eng-en, translated by Arthur Waley, London, George
Allen & Unwin Limited, 1942, pp. 267–8.)

17. The art of fortunetelling by interpreting dreams, called
"Oneiromancy," has a long history in China. It was considered
a lesser art of making prognostications as compared with
such methods of divination as the use of oracle bones and
horoscope reading. However, in Chinese novels and notebooks, stories of dream interpretation are so abundant as to
suggest that the custom has always been very popular among
the people. An authoritative book on the subject was published in the late Ming, called *Meng-chan i-chih* 夢占逸旨 by
Chen Shih-yüan 陳士元. Perhaps the Chinese dream interpretation idea could be regarded as a precursor to the Freudian
investigation of the subconscious mind.

The art of fortunetelling by dissecting written characters
called "Glyphomancy" is only possible in a culture that has
an ideographic language. Many unemployed scholars earned
a meager living by setting up roadside stalls to make prognostications by dissecting words picked by clients at random.
However, it is generally considered more of a con game to
swindle the ignorant than a serious attempt at telling the
future. (See Joseph Needham, *Science & Civilization in
China,* Cambridge University Press, 1962, Vol. II, p. 364 and
J. J. M. deGroot, "On Chinese Divination by Dissecting
Chinese Characters," in *T'oung Pao* 通報, 1890, Vol. I, p. 239.)

18. Han Yü 韓愈 (768–824), one of the eight literary masters
of the T'ang-Sung Period. During the reign of Teh-tsung (r.
780–805), Han Yü and two other officials, Departmental

Secretaries Chang Shu and Li Fang-shu were exiled for offending a powerful minister in the court. Han was demoted to be the magistrate of Yang-shan in Kuangtung and Chang the magistrate of Liu-chou in Kwangsi. Three years later, a general amnesty was proclaimed following the ascendancy of a new emperor, Hsien-tsung (r. 806–820), to the throne. While waiting for the imperial order to go back to the capital, Han and Chang met in Pin-chou, Hunan where this poem was supposedly written. The night of the fifteenth of the eighth moon is traditionally the night of the harvest festival when the moon is fullest and brightest.

A literary translation of this poem would require footnotes lengthier than the poem itself. The general idea of this poem may be rendered as follows:

Wispy clouds have unfurled to cover the milkyway. A gentle breeze has filled the space brightened by the moonlight. The current near the sandbar flows silently. I raise my cup to entreat you to sing. Your song, however, is piquant and the lyric bitter. Before you finish your song my tears pour down my cheeks like rain. The meaning of your song is loud and clear: 'The water of Tung-ting Lake reaches the edge of heaven; the pinacles of Mt. Nine Doubts pierce through the clouds. Dragons and water snakes frolic amidst the waves and monkeys and beasts wail in the forest. I reached the exiled office after risking my life countless times. I keep my silence and lead a placid existence as if I were a fugitive. Getting up from the bed I fear snake bite; taking my meals I am afraid of poisoning. The place is damp and the air odorous. Yesterday someone beat the drum in front of the prefect's office, proclaiming the ascendancy of the new emperor to the throne. There will be able ministers to assist the new sovereign. The patent of a general amnesty travelled a thousand *li* a day. All were pardoned except those who received the death penalty. Officials demoted or exiled were ordered to return. Condemned persons would be rehabilitated and the wrongly accused would have their good names restored. The prefect has sent in the names of the pardoned, but the list was suppressed by the governor. Oh, how malign is my fate; I have to be reconciled with the prospect of living in the southern wilderness. Minor officials like me receive scanty attention and physical beating is not spared when blamed. Others have embarked on their homeward journeys. Why is it so difficult for me to squeeze through the gate of opportunity?' I implored him to stop singing the pathetic song and listen to what I had to say: 'My song is different from what you have just sung. There is no better moonlit night than tonight. Everything in life is predestined by Heaven and no amount of remorse is going to help. Refusing to drink when offered is incompatible with the proper enjoyment of the moonlight.'

19. Liu Yung 柳永 (fl. 1034) was a Bohemian poet who loved the company of courtesans. All his poems possess a sense of *joie de vivre* and describe the conviviality of mixed gatherings. Here, the author alludes to the word "her" in Liu's poem as "motherland"—a stretch of imagination permitted only with poetic license.

20. This is the main theme of the book—the utter futility of the re-education process that the author has gone through in the cadre school. If it is meant as an indictment of the Cultural Revolution itself, it is not a direct and explicit one. Her descriptions give the impression that the cadre school was not altogether an inhumane place, albeit an ineffective one for achieving its avowed purposes. There are many things that have been intentionally avoided in her story. Even the tragic suicide of her son-in-law was glossed over with only a brief mention. Chinese intellectuals have long since learned to cooperate with the inevitable. It is this attitude that perhaps has saved the author from severe persecution which was the common lot of her peers and enabled this book to be published.